"PHILOSOPHY IS EVERYBODY'S BUSINESS . . .

Aristotle's thinking began with common sense, but it did not end there. It went much further. It added to and surrounded common sense with insights and understandings that are not common at all. His understanding of things goes deeper than ours and sometimes soars higher. It is, in a word, *uncommon* common sense."

—from the Introduction

"With chapters on 'Productive Ideas and Know-How,' 'How to Pursue Happiness,' and 'What Others Have a Right to Expect from Us,' this is a 'self-help' book in the best sense of the term. . . . The Aristotelian wisdom Adler affords us goes far beyond anything all the Norman Vincent Peales, Michael Kordas, and Wayne W. Dyers combined have to offer. Above all, Adler once again demonstrates that philosophy, real philosophy, can actually be useful."

—*Chicago Tribune Book World*

D0816079

Bantam Books by Mortimer J. Adler

ARISTOTLE FOR EVERYBODY
HOW TO THINK ABOUT GOD

ARISTOTLE
FOR
EVERYBODY

DIFFICULT THOUGHT
MADE EASY

Mortimer J. Adler

BANTAM BOOKS
TORONTO · NEW YORK · LONDON · SYDNEY

ARISTOTLE FOR EVERYBODY

*A Bantam Book / published by arrangement with
Macmillan Publishing Co., Inc.*

PRINTING HISTORY

*Macmillan edition published May 1978
7 printings through November 1979
Bantam edition / December 1980*

ISBN 0-553-13995-9

Published simultaneously in the United States and Canada

PRINTED IN THE UNITED STATES OF AMERICA

0 9 8 7 6 5 4 3

Contents

Part IV   Man the Knower

Part V   Difficult Philosophical Questions

Preface

When the idea for this book first occurred to me, I thought of entitling it *The Children's Aristotle* or *Aristotle for Children*. But those titles would not have accurately conveyed the audience for whom this simple, easy-to-read exposition of Aristotle's common-sense philosophy is intended. The audience, I felt, was *everybody*—of any age, from twelve or fourteen years old upward. Hence the title chosen, and the subtitle "Difficult Thought Made Easy," together with the statement that this book is an *introduction to common sense*.

When I say "everybody," I mean everybody *except* professional philosophers; in other words, everybody of ordinary experience and intelligence unspoiled by the sophistication and specialization of academic thought. Nevertheless, I have added an Epilogue which students of philosophy who come upon this book may find useful as a guide to the reading of Aristotle's own works on the subjects covered in this book.

My two sons, Douglas and Philip (thirteen and eleven, respectively), read portions of the manuscript as it came from my typewriter last summer in Aspen. I am grateful to them for their enthusiasm and their suggestions.

I wish also to express my gratitude to Rosemary Barnes, who read and criticized the whole manuscript at that time, as well as to my colleagues at the Institute for Philosophical Research who gave me the benefit of their advice—John Van Doren, Otto Bird, and Charles Van Doren. At a later date, just before the manuscript went into type, my wife, Caroline, read the whole of it and made suggestions for its improvement, for which I am grateful.

As always, I am very much in debt to my editorial secretary, Marlys Allen, for her tireless efforts at every stage in the production of this book.

MORTIMER J. ADLER

Chicago
December 28, 1977

Introduction

Why Aristotle?

Why for everybody?

And why is an exposition of Aristotle for everybody an introduction to common sense?

I can answer these three questions better after I have answered one other. Why philosophy? Why should everyone learn how to think philosophically—how to ask the kind of searching questions that children and philosophers ask and that philosophers sometimes answer?

I have long been of the opinion that philosophy is everybody's business—but not in order to get more information about the world, our society, and ourselves. For that purpose, it would be better to turn to the natural and the social sciences and to history. It is in another way that philosophy is useful—to help us to understand things we already know, understand them better than we now understand them. That is why I think everyone should learn how to think philosophically.

For that purpose there is no better teacher than Aristotle. I do not hesitate to recommend him as the teacher to begin with. The only other teacher that I might have chosen is Plato, but in my judgment he is second best. Plato raised almost all the questions that everyone should face; Aristotle raised them too and, in addition, gave us clearer answers to them. Plato taught Aristotle how to think philosophically, but Aristotle learned the lesson so well that he is the better teacher for all of us.

Since we are concerned with learning how to think the way Aristotle did, what Aristotle thought is more important than who he was or when and how he lived. The centuries and the changes that separate him from us may make the conditions of his life and the society in which he lived appear strange to us; but, as I will try to explain, they do not make either the style or the content of his thinking strange to us.

Aristotle was born in 384 B.C. in the Macedonian town of Stagira on the north coast of the Aegean Sea. His father was a physician in the court of the King of Macedonia. The King's grandson became Alexander the Great, to whom Aristotle later became both tutor and friend.

At the age of eighteen, Aristotle took up residence in Athens and enrolled in Plato's Academy as a student of philosophy. It was not long before Plato found Aristotle a troublesome student who questioned what he taught and openly disagreed with him. When Plato died, and Alexander became the ruler of Greece, Aristotle opened his own school, the Lyceum. That was in 335 B.C.

The Lyceum had a fine library, an extensive collection of maps, and a zoo in which Aristotle collected specimens of animal life. It has been said that some of these were sent to him by Alexander from the countries he conquered. When Alexander died in 323 B.C., Aristotle exiled himself from Athens to one of the Aegean islands. He died there a year later at the age of 63.

Aristotle lived in a society in which the citizens had free time to enjoy the pursuits of leisure because they had slaves to take care of their estates and to do menial work. It was also a society in which women occupied an inferior position. Plato, in projecting the institutions of an ideal state, proposed that all political offices, except that of military leader, should be open to women, because he regarded men and women as essentially equal; but Aristotle accepted the more conventional view of his day concerning the inferiority of women.

I shall have more to say in a later chapter about Aristotle's views with regard to slavery and to women. Here I want to say at once that my use of the words "man," "men," and "mankind" in their generic sense to stand for human beings of both genders, and not just for the male portion of the population, is in no way an indication that I share Aristotle's view about women. On the contrary, with regard to this point, I am a Platonist.

There may be some persons who regard Aristotle's antiquity as a disadvantage. They may feel that it would be much better to select as a teacher someone alive today—someone acquainted with the world in which we live, someone who knows what modern science has discovered about that world. I do not agree with them.

Though Aristotle was a Greek who lived twenty-five centuries ago, he was sufficiently acquainted with the main outlines of the world in which we live to talk about it as if he were alive today. As an aid to our being able to think philosophically, Aristotle would not be a better teacher even if he were acquainted with everything that modern scientists know.

In an effort to understand nature, society, and man, Aristotle began where everyone should begin—with what he already knew in the light of his ordinary, commonplace experience. Beginning there, his thinking used notions that all of us possess, not because we were taught them in school, but because they are the common stock of human thought about anything and everything.

We sometimes refer to these notions as our common sense about things. They are notions that we have formed as a result of the common experience we have in the course of our daily lives—experiences we have without any effort of inquiry on our part, experiences we all have simply because we are awake and conscious. In addition, these common notions are notions we are able to express in the common words we employ in everyday speech.

Forgive me for repeating the word "common" so many times. I cannot avoid doing so, and I have to lay stress on that word because what it means lies at the heart of my argument. Not everything is common. There are many things we call our own, but there are other things that we recognize as not exclusively ours. We share them with others, such as a book that our friends have read or a motion picture some of us have enjoyed, or a house that all the members of the family share when they live in it together.

The things we share are common. There are many things that different groups of people share. There are fewer things that we all share and are common to all of us, simply because we are all human. It is in this last, all-embracing sense of the word "common" that I refer to common experiences and common notions, or common sense, as common.

Our common-sense notions are expressed by such words as "thing," "body," "mind," "change," "cause," "part," "whole," "one," "many," and so on. Most of us have been using these words and notions for a long time—since we were quite young. We started to use them in order to talk about experiences that all of us have had—of things moving or remaining at rest, of plants growing, or animals being born and dying, of sitting down and getting up, of aches and pains, of going to sleep, dreaming, and waking up, of feeding and exercising our bodies, and of making up our minds.

I could enlarge this list of our common experiences, just as I could enlarge the list of the common words we use and the common notions we have. But even without the additions that could be made, it should be clear that the words, experiences, and notions I have mentioned are all common—not exclusively yours, or mine, or anyone else's.

In contrast, the things that scientists observe in their laboratories or that explorers observe on their expeditions are very special experiences. We may learn about them from their reports, but, as a rule, we do not experience them ourselves.

Human beings have learned a great deal since Aristotle's day, mainly through the discoveries of modern science. Applied science has created a world and a way of life very different from his world and his way of life. He did not have an automobile, could not talk on the telephone, never saw what can be seen through a microscope or a telescope, did not have a close view of the surface of the moon, and never heard a description of its surface by men walking on it. But Aristotle had the same common experiences in his day that we have in ours. The kind of thinking he did about them enabled him to understand them better than most of us do.

That and that alone is the reason he can help us to understand these common experiences better and help us to understand ourselves and our lives, as well as the world and the society in which we live, even though our way of life, our world, and our society are different from his.

Aristotle's thinking *began* with common sense, but it did not *end* there. It went much further. It added to and surrounded common sense with insights and understandings that are not common at all. His understanding of things goes deeper than ours and sometimes soars higher. It is, in a word, *uncommon* common sense.

That is his great contribution to all of us. What I am going to try to do in this book is to make his *uncommon* common sense easier to understand. If it becomes easier to understand, it might even become less uncommon.

PART I

MAN THE
PHILOSOPHICAL
ANIMAL

1

Philosophical Games

Many of us have played two games without realizing we were on the way to becoming philosophical. One is called "Animal, Vegetable, Mineral"; the other, "Twenty Questions."

Both games consist in asking questions. However, that is not what makes them philosophical games; it is what lies behind the questions—a set of categories, a scheme of classification. Classifying things, placing them in this or that category, is a familiar process. Everyone does it at one time or another—shopkeepers when they take stock of what is on their shelves, librarians when they catalogue books, secretaries when they file letters or documents. But when the objects to be classified are the contents of the physical world, or the even-larger universe that includes the physical world, then philosophy enters the picture.

The two games—"Animal, Vegetable, Mineral" and "Twenty Questions"—are sometimes played as if they were the same game. That occurs when the first of the twenty questions to be asked is "Animal, vegetable, or mineral?" in order to find out whether the object being thought of falls into one of these three large categories, or classes, of physical things. But only some of the objects we can think about are physical things. If, for example, the object decided on was a geometrical figure, such as a circle, or a number, such as the square root of minus one, or if it happened to be one of the Greek gods, such as Zeus, Apollo, or Athena, asking whether the object in question was animal, vegetable, or mineral would not—or, at least, should not—get an answer.

The game of twenty questions, when it is not begun by asking "Animal, vegetable, or mineral?" is concerned with discovering any object that can be thought about by anybody. It is not limited to objects that are physical things. Of the two games, it is the more likely to engage us in philosophical thought without our being aware of it. To become aware of it, we need Aristotle's help.

Classifying was one of the skills in which Aristotle excelled. Another was his skill in asking questions. Philosophical thought began with the asking of questions—questions that can be answered on the basis of our ordinary, everyday experience and with some reflection about that experience that results in a sharpening and refinement of our common sense.

Animal, vegetable, and mineral is a rough-and-ready, three-fold division of things we find in the physical world. But we use the word "mineral" loosely when we use it to stand for all the physical things that fall on one side of the line that divides living organisms from inanimate things—rosebushes or mice from sticks or stones. All inanimate things are not minerals, such as gold or silver that we dig from deposits in the earth. Some are rock formations found on the earth's surface or in its interior; some are other forms of matter in liquid or gaseous states.

In the category of nonliving or inanimate bodies that is loosely covered by the term "mineral," Aristotle would have to distinguish between elementary and composite bodies. An elementary body, according to Aristotle, is one that consists in a single kind of matter—gold, for example, or copper or zinc. In contrast, a composite body is one that is composed of two or more different kinds of matter, such as brass, which is a mixture of copper and zinc. But, for Aristotle, the more important distinction is the one that divides living from nonliving things.

What differentiates all living organisms from inert bodies, whether they are elementary or composite bodies? From our ordinary experience of living organisms, we know that they all have certain common characteristics. They take nourishment; they grow; they reproduce.

Among living organisms, what differentiates plants from animals? Again, from our ordinary experience, we know that animals have certain common characteristics that plants lack. They are not rooted in the earth like plants; they have the ability to move from place to place by their own means of locomotion. They do not draw their nourishment from the air and from the soil as plants do. In addition, most animals have sense organs.

The line that divides inert bodies from living organisms sometimes leaves us wondering on which side of the line a particular thing belongs. This is also true of the line that divides plants from animals. For example, some plants appear to have sensitivity even though they do not have sense organs like eyes and ears. Some animals, such as shellfish, seem to lack the power of locomotion; like plants they appear to be rooted in one spot.

In classifying physical things as inanimate bodies, plants, and animals, Aristotle was aware that his division of all physical things into these three large classes did not exclude borderline cases—things that in a certain respect appear to belong on one side of the dividing line and that, in another respect, appear to belong on the other side. He recognized that in the world of bodies, the transition from things lifeless to living things and from plant life to animal life is gradual and not a clear-cut, all-or-none affair.

Nevertheless, Aristotle persisted in thinking that the differences between living and nonliving bodies and between plants and animals separated them into quite different kinds of things. His reason for holding this view was as follows.

If we did not, in the first place, recognize and understand the clear-cut distinction between a stone and a mouse, we would never find ourselves puzzled by whether something difficult to classify was a living or a nonliving thing. Similarly, if we did not recognize the clear-cut distinction between a rosebush and a horse, we would never wonder whether a given specimen of living organism was a plant or an animal.

Just as animals are a special kind of living organism because they perform functions that plants do not, so for a similar reason are human beings a special kind of animal. They perform certain functions that no other animals perform, such as asking general questions and seeking answers to them by observation and by thought. That is why Aristotle called human beings rational animals—questioning and thinking animals, able to engage in philosophical thought.

There may be animals that appear to straddle the borderline that divides humans and nonhumans. Porpoises and chimpanzees, it has recently been learned, have enough intelligence to engage in rudimentary forms of communication. But they do not appear to ask themselves or one another questions about the nature of things, and they do not appear to try, by one means or another, to discover the answers for themselves. We may speak of such animals as almost human, but we do not include them as members of the human race.

Each distinct kind of thing, Aristotle thought, has a nature that distinguishes it from all the others. What differentiates one class of things from everything else defines the nature possessed by every individual thing that belongs to that class. When we speak of human nature, for example, we are simply saying that all human beings have certain characteristics and that these characteristics differentiate them from other animals, from plants, and from inanimate things.

Aristotle's scheme of classification arranged the five main classes of physical things in an ascending order. He placed elementary and composite bodies at the bottom of the scale. Each of the higher classes is higher because it possesses the characteristics of the class below and, in addition, has certain distinguishing characteristics that the class below does not have.

In the scale of natural things, the animate is a higher form of existence than the inanimate; animals are a higher form of life than plants; and human life is the highest form of life on earth.

All living organisms, like all inanimate bodies, occupy space and have weight, but in addition, as we have noted, they eat, grow, and reproduce. Because they arc living organisms, animals, like plants, perform these vital functions, but they also perform certain functions that plants do not. At the top of the scale are human beings who perform all the vital functions performed by other animals and who, in addition, have the ability to seek knowledge by asking and answering questions and the ability to think philosophically.

Of course, it can be said that many of the higher animals think, and even that computers think. Nor is it true that only humans have intelligence. Intelligence in varying degrees is to be found throughout the animal world, just as it is to be found in varying degrees in members of the human race. But the special kind of thinking that gives rise to asking and answering philosophical questions distinguishes humans from other animals. No other animal plays philosophical games.

In the world of physical things that Aristotle divides into five large classes, the word "body" names the one, all-embracing class. There is no more inclusive class of which bodies are a subclass. Every *thing* in the physical world is a *body* of one kind or another.

Can we go to the opposite extreme and find a subclass of bodies at which we must stop because we are unable to divide it any further into smaller subclasses? Is the human species such a subclass of animals?

Faced with that question, most of us probably think at once of different races or varieties of mankind—differentiated by skin color, by facial characteristics, by head shape, and so on. Why do not such characteristics divide human beings into different kinds or subclasses?

In this connection, Aristotle made an important distinction. Not all the characteristics of a thing, he said, define its nature or essence. As we have already seen, Aristotle thought man should be defined as rational—or philosophical—animal. Being able to ask questions about the what, the why, and the wherefore of things is what makes anyone a human being, not the skin color, the snub nose, the straight hair, or the shape of the head.

We can, of course, divide human beings into an endless variety of subclasses—tall or short, fat or thin, white or black, strong or weak, and so on. But although such differences may be used to distinguish one subgroup of human beings from another, they cannot be used, according to Aristotle, to exclude any of these subgroups from the human race. What is even more important, it cannot be said that the members of one subgroup are more or less human than the members of another.

In other words, the differences between one subclass of human beings and another are superficial or minor, as compared with the basic or major differences that separate human beings from other animals. Aristotle called the superficial or minor differences accidental; the basic or major differences he regarded as essential.

Human beings and brute animals are essentially different; tall human beings and short ones, fat human beings and thin ones, are accidentally different. It is only in this way that one human being differs from another. We are all animals of the same kind, but one individual may have more and another individual less of this or that human characteristic. Such individual differences are much less important than the one thing that unites all men and women—their common humanity, which is the one respect in which all human beings are equal.

2

The Great Divide

Aristotle's division of physical things into inanimate bodies and living organisms, and his division of living organisms into plants, animals, and human beings, do not exhaust his scheme of classification or his set of categories.

Think, for example, of Wellington's horse at the Battle of Waterloo or of Julius Caesar crossing the Rubicon. Think of Shakespeare's Hamlet, the Loch Ness monster, or the angel Gabriel. Think of the odor of roses in full bloom, the color of a ripe tomato, Newton's theory of gravitation, or God.

None of these is a physical thing that exists now as animal, vegetable, or mineral. Wellington's horse and Julius Caesar existed in the past, but they exist no longer. Shakespeare's Hamlet is a fictitious person, not a real one. The existence of the Loch Ness monster is highly questionable. As for the odor of roses in full bloom, the angel Gabriel, Newton's theory of gravitation, and God, none of these fall under any of the headings that cover bodies that either exist or have existed in the physical world.

The universe of objects that can be thought of is much larger than the physical world—the world of bodies, either those now in existence or those that have existed in the past. It includes the world of bodies, but it also includes much else besides. The line that divides bodies from everything is the great divide.

What is left when we put the whole physical word to one side? What belongs to the other half of the all-embracing universe of objects that we can think about? I am not going to try to give an exhaustive enumeration of the kinds of objects that are *not* bodies, but here at least are some of the possible kinds:

—mathematical objects, such as triangles and square roots
—imaginary or fictitious characters, such as Shakespeare's Hamlet or Mark Twain's Huckleberry Finn
—disembodied or unembodied spirits of all sorts, including ghosts and angels
—gods or God when divine beings are thought of as not having bodies
—mythological beings, such as centaurs and mermaids
—minds that are able to think up the kind of questions we have been asking
—ideas or theories that minds think with

I am fully aware that this enumeration of possible objects of thought raises many questions. Do such objects exist, in any sense of that word? If they do, how does their existence differ from the existence of bodies? What does it mean to call them possibilities? Are there any objects of thought that are impossibilities? If minds are not bodies, what is their relationship to bodies?

I will try to answer some of these questions—with Aristotle's help—in later chapters of this book. Some are difficult philosophical questions that I will postpone until the very end. For the moment, asking them serves the purpose of calling attention to the larger universe of which the physical world is but a part, even though the world of bodies may be the only one that really exists.

Staying with that world, we must consider another

distinction made by Aristotle. We need it to handle the question about the odor of roses in full bloom or the color of a ripe tomato. Roses and tomatoes are bodies, they are plants, but their odor and their color are not. Considering the physical world, Aristotle drew a line that divides its constituents into two major kinds. On the one side of the line, he placed *bodies;* on the other side, their *characteristics* or *attributes,* such as their odors or colors.

In our everyday speech, we ordinarily make the same distinction. We do not speak of the size and weight of a stone as if it were a body. I would not ask you to hand me the stone's size or weight, for I know that you must hand me the stone in order for me to feel its size or weight.

We can think of the stone's size or weight without thinking of the stone, but we cannot change the stone's size or weight without changing the stone. If the stone is lying in a pile of stones, we can take it from the pile and leave the other stones behind, but we cannot take the stone's size or weight away from it and leave the stone behind.

What belongs to a body in the way in which the stone's size or weight belongs to it is, according to Aristotle, something that has its existence in a thing (as the stone's weight exists in the stone), but does not exist in and of itself (as the stone exists).

A physical thing, a body, may belong to a collection of things from which it can be removed—as one stone can be taken from a pile of stones. But each of the stones in the pile exists in and of itself, even when it exists in a collection of stones. That is not true of the stone's size or weight. Sizes and weights do not exist in and of themselves. They are always the sizes and weights of physical things, and they cease to exist when the bodies in which they exist cease to exist.

Another way of grasping this basic distinction between physical things and their attributes is to consider how things change. A stone with a rough surface can be polished and made smooth. A stone that is almost round in shape can be made perfectly round. While we are changing a stone's attributes, we are dealing with one and the same stone. It is not another stone, but the same stone altered.

If it did not remain the same stone while becoming different in this or that respect, it could not be said to have changed from being rough to being smooth, or from being larger to being smaller. When we understand this, we understand Aristotle's reason for saying that a physical thing is that which remains what it is (this individual stone) while at the same time being subject to change in one respect or another (in size or weight, shape, color, or texture).

The attributes of bodies, unlike bodies themselves, are never subject to change. Roughness never becomes smoothness; green never becomes red. It is the rough *stone* that becomes smooth; the green *tomato* that becomes red when it ripens. Physical things, in short, are changeable. Physical attributes are not changeable; they are the respects in which physical things change.

Aristotle attempted to make a complete enumeration of the attributes that physical things have. Its completeness may be questioned, but the attributes he names are ones we are all acquainted with in common experience, especially those that are the principal respects in which things change:

— in quantity, when they increase or decrease in weight or size
— in quality, when they alter in shape, color, or texture
— in place or position, when they move from here to there

A thing has other attributes, such as the relationships in which it stands to other things, the actions it performs, the results of its being acted on, the time of its coming into existence, the duration of its existence, and the time of its ceasing to exist.

Of all the attributes that a physical thing has, the most important are those that it has throughout its existence and with respect to which it does not change as long as it exists. These permanent attributes make it the kind of thing it is. For example, it is a permanent attribute of salt that it dissolves in water; a permanent attribute of certain metals that they are conductors of electricity; a permanent attribute of mammals that they give birth to living offspring and suckle their young.

Such attributes not only make a thing the special kind of thing it is, they also differentiate one kind of thing from another. Being able to ask questions of the sort we have been asking is a permanent attribute of rational animals that differentiates us from other mammals. Rational animals are, of course, bodies. They are physical things, but not only physical things.

We recognize this fact in our use of the word "person." We call human beings persons. We do not call spiders, snakes, sharks or birds persons. When we treat our pet cat or dog as if it were a person, we treat it as if it were human—or almost human. Objects that we regard as mere things, we do not treat in the same manner.

Up to this point, the word "thing" has been used to refer to physical things—to bodies. Now the word "thing" has been used in contrast to the word "person." It is a troublesome word. Its meaning is sometimes so broad that it refers to any possible object of thought—not only to existent physical things, but also to their attributes as well, and to objects that do not exist, objects that may never have existed, and even objects that cannot possibly exist. Sometimes the word "thing" narrowly applies only to bodies that now exist in the physical world, bodies that have existed there in the past, or bodies that can exist there in the future.

Using the same word in a variety of senses is often unavoidable. In the case of the most important words we use, especially words we use in ordinary everyday speech, it is almost impossible not to do so. Aristotle frequently called attention to the different senses in which he found it necessary to use the same word. When we think about our experience as he did, we must also pay attention to the different senses of the words we use.

Human beings are physical things in one sense of that word and not in another when we call them persons, not things. As physical things, as bodies, they have the three dimensions with which we are all acquainted. As persons, they also have three dimensions, which are quite different.

3

Man's Three Dimensions

Regarding ourselves simply as bodies—or merely
as physical things—I would say that our three dimensions, like the three dimensions of any other body, are
length, breadth, and height. That is the way in which
any body occupies space.

While, as bodies, we are physical things like all
other bodies, we are, as we have just seen, the special
kind of thing—the only kind of thing—that is called a
person. What are our three dimensions as persons, not
just bodies?

In space, a dimension is a direction in which I can
move. I can move my hand from left to right, from
front to back, from up to down. Like spatial dimensions, personal dimensions are also directions—directions in which I, as a person, can act as a human
being. I am sure that we have only three dimensions as
physical bodies, but I cannot be as sure that we have
only three dimensions as active human beings—only
three directions in which our activities can take us.

However, I think that the three dimensions I shall
name represent three very important directions that human activity can take. There may be others, but I

15

doubt if there are any as important as these. The three are making, doing, and knowing.

In the first of these three dimensions, making, we have man the artist or artisan—the producer of all sorts of things: shoes, ships, and houses, books, music, and paintings. It is not just when human beings produce statues or paintings that we should call them artists. That is much too restricted a use of the word art. Anything in the world that is artificial rather than natural is a work of art—something man-made.

In the second of these dimensions, doing, we have man the moral and social being—someone who can do right or wrong, someone who, by what he or she does or does not do, either achieves happiness or fails to achieve it, someone who finds it necessary to associate with other human beings in order to do what, as a human being, he or she feels impelled to do.

In the third dimension, knowing, we have man as learner, acquiring knowledge of all sorts—not only about nature, not only about the society of which human beings are a part, not only about human nature, but also about knowledge itself.

In all three of these dimensions, man is a thinker, but the kind of thinking he does in order to make things differs from the kind of thinking he does in order to act morally and socially. Both kinds of thinking differ from the kind of thinking a human being does in order just to know—to know just for the sake of knowing.

Aristotle was very much concerned with the differences that distinguish these three kinds of thinking. He used the term "productive thinking" to describe the kind of thinking that man engages in as a maker; "practical thinking" to describe the kind that he engages in as a doer; and "speculative" or "theoretical thinking" to describe the kind he engages in as a knower.

This threefold division of the kinds of thinking can be found in Aristotle's books. Some of them, such as his books on moral and political philosophy, are concerned with practical thinking and with man as a doer—as an individual living his own life and trying to make it as good as possible, and also as a member of society, associated with other human beings and cooperating with them. Some of these books, such as the ones on natural philosophy, are concerned with theoretical thinking about the whole physical world, including man as a part of that world, and man's mind and knowledge as well.

He wrote a treatise about man as a maker, but that book deals only with man as a maker of poetry, music, and paintings. He entitled it *Poetics* because the Greek word from which we get the word "poetry" means making—making anything, not just the kind of objects that entertain us and that give us pleasure when we enjoy them. Men and women produce an extraordinary variety of useful things, things we use in our daily lives, such as the clothes we wear, the houses we live in, the furniture in those houses, and the implements needed to make such things.

The more general treatment of man as a maker, particularly man as a maker of useful physical things, we find in the books that Aristotle wrote about nature—his books of natural philosophy. In his effort to understand the phenomena of nature, Aristotle frequently resorted to comparisons between the way men produce things and the way nature works. His understanding of what is involved in human making helped him—and it will help us—to understand the workings of nature.

That is why I am going to begin, in Part II of this book, with making as a dimension of human activity. After that, in Part III, I am going to deal with the dimension of human activity in which man is a moral and social being. And finally, in Part IV, I will come to man as a knower, postponing to the last the most difficult questions that we have to consider—questions about the human mind and knowledge itself.

The most challenging words in anyone's vocabulary are three words that name the universal values that elicit respect and evoke wonder. They are truth, goodness, and beauty—or the true, the good, and the beautiful. These three values pertain to the three dimensions of human activity.

In the sphere of making, we are concerned with beauty, or, to say the least, with trying to produce things that are well made. In the sphere of doing, as individuals and as members of society, we are concerned with good and evil, right and wrong. In the sphere of knowing, we are concerned with truth.

PART II

MAN THE MAKER

4

Aristotle's Crusoe

If Aristotle had written the story of Robinson Crusoe, the moral of the tale would have been different.

The story most of us have read celebrates Crusoe's ingenuity in solving the problem of how to live securely and comfortably on the island where he found himself a castaway after a shipwreck. It also celebrates his virtues—his courage and his foresight. It is a story of man's conquest of nature, his mastery and control over it.

For Aristotle, the island would have represented Nature, nature with a capital *N*, nature untouched by humans. The works of nature—the seeding of trees and bushes, the growth of plants, the birth and death of animals, the shifting of sands, the wearing away of rocks, the formation of caves—had been going on long before Crusoe's arrival. Aristotle would have viewed the changes that Crusoe brought about as a way of understanding the changes that had taken place without him. For him, the story would not have been a story of man *against* nature, but an account of man *working with* nature.

When we try to understand something that is difficult to understand, a good common-sense rule is to start out with something easier to understand in order to see if that helps us overcome the difficulties. What is more understandable may throw some light on what is less understandable. Human beings should be able to understand what goes on when they make something or change something. That is less difficult to understand than what goes on in nature when human beings are not in the picture. Understanding works of art may, therefore, help us to understand the workings of nature.

I suggested, in the preceding chapter, that in its broadest meaning the phrase "work of art" covers everything that is manmade. Let's reconsider that. Is everything produced by human beings artificial, not natural? When parents produce children, are the children artificial? Are they works of art? If you say no, as I think you should, then we have not yet succeeded in correctly drawing the line that divides the artificial from the natural.

Suppose that lightning strikes a tree in the dense forest. The tree is split in half; branches are cut off. The burning of some of them sets off a forest fire. The forest fire and all the other changes that result from the lightning's stroke are all natural, are they not?

But a person, walking through the woods, carelessly throws away a lighted cigarette. It sets the dry leaves of the underbrush on fire, and the woods are consumed in flames. That forest fire was caused by a human being, as the first one was caused by lightning. The first one was a work of nature. Was the second a work of man—something artificial, not natural?

Suppose, however, that the individual in the woods had not dropped a lighted cigarette. Suppose he had gathered dry twigs and leaves and heaped them in a mound that he surrounded with small stones. Then, lighting a match, he set fire to them in order to cook his lunch. We would ordinarily say, would we not, that he had *built* a fire. Would the fire he built be a work of art, unlike the fire set off by the careless dropping of a lighted cigarette?

Before you answer that question too quickly,

remember that fire itself is something natural. It does not need a human being to make it happen. In fact, when man does make it happen, what does he make— the fire itself or does he merely cause it to happen at a certain time and place, as the man walking through the woods caused it to happen at the spot where he decided to cook lunch?

One more example to consider: lightning split the tree and cut off some of its branches. Men can do that, too, with axes and saws; and they do it when they engage in lumbering in order to obtain the wood they need to build houses, or to make chairs and tables. You understand that the houses men build are products of art, not of nature—artificial, not natural. Building a house, then, is not quite the same as building a fire, for you cannot be quite so sure that the fire a man builds is artificial, not natural.

What is the difference between the man-made house—or the man-made chair or table—and the man-made fire? Or between the tree's branches that are cut off by lightning and the tree's branches that are cut down by lumberjacks? Or between the fire built by the picnicker in order to cook his lunch and the fire caused by the man tramping through the woods who carelessly dropped a lighted cigarette?

Let's start with the easiest question first. The fire caused by the lighted cigarette was accidental rather than intentional. It was not for a purpose that some human being had in mind. It resulted from human carelessness—even mindlessness—rather than from careful planning and foresight. The absence of any human purpose, planning, or foresight puts it on the natural side of the line that divides the natural from the artificial.

It was man-caused but not man-made. It resulted from something that a human being did, but man is a part of nature just as much as lightning is. Not everything that results from human behavior is a human production of a work of art.

Now, what of the man-made fire, deliberately built for the purpose of cooking lunch, and the man-made house, deliberately built for the purpose of providing shelter? Here neither humanly-brought-about result is accidental. Purpose and planning are certainly involved in both. So far, at least, both belong on the artificial side of the line that divides the natural from the artificial. What, then, is the difference between them?

One difference is clear immediately. Fires happen in nature when men are not present, but houses do not. Men can help nature produce fires by lighting matches and setting dry leaves and twigs aflame. But when human beings build houses rather than fires, they are not helping nature produce them. In the one case, we said before, men do not make fire itself, but they make fires happen at a certain time and place. In the other case, men do make houses.

The house that Robinson Crusoe built after he had rescued some tools from the shipwreck was something that he and he alone produced, not something he just made happen at a certain time and place. Except for his being on the island, no houses would have ever happened, as fires might have happened as a result of bolts of lightning.

One more question remains. We have so far decided that Crusoe's house, planned and produced for a purpose, is a work of art, not of nature, something artificial, not natural. But is it entirely artificial—wholly a human creation? The Bible tells us that before God created the world there was nothing, and that God's creation of the world brought something out of nothing. Did Crusoe bring something out of nothing when he built his house?

Hardly. He built it out of the wood he had obtained from chopping down trees with his ax, cutting off branches with his saw, and smoothing them with his plane. The wood that went into the building of the house came from nature. It was there to begin with. So, too, was the iron out of which nails had been formed, nails that Crusoe recovered along with tools in the carpenter's chest that floated ashore after the shipwreck. The house, made out of wood and nails, was indeed made by Crusoe, not by nature, but it was made out of natural materials. That is also true of all the tools that Crusoe had the good luck to be able to use.

Let's not forget the children that parents produce. We have already decided that children are natural products, not artificial—not works of art. Is that because they are sometimes accidental products rather than intentional ones?

Sometimes, we know, children are the result of carelessness or thoughtlessness, and are as unexpected as they are unplanned for. But even when children are wanted and planned for, even when some thought is involved in begetting them, and even when, with some luck, parents help nature produce children at a certain time and place, they are not like the fire that the picnicker helped nature to produce or the house that Crusoe built out of materials provided by nature.

Why not? For the time being, let us be satisfied with the answer suggested above. Children, like the offspring of other animals, can certainly happen without any thought, planning, or purpose. That is not true of anything we would call a work of art or artificial. But just as human beings can make fires happen by knowing something about how fires happen in nature, so, too, can human beings make children happen by knowing something about how the procreation of offspring happens in nature.

When they are totally ignorant of that, then their offspring are entirely accidental. But when they have such knowledge, the having of offspring is, partly at least, the result of planning and purpose.

We have surveyed a lot of happenings and productions, and we have compared the differences between them in order to see if we can place each on one or the other side of the line that divides the natural and the artificial. Before we go on, it might be a good idea to summarize what we have learned.

First, we decided that fire itself is something entirely natural. The particular fire a man purposely builds at a certain time and place is an artificial happening—something that would not have happened had not some human being caused it to happen then and there.

Second, the artificiality of the fire the picnicker built in order to make lunch differs from the artificiality of the house that Crusoe built in order to provide himself with shelter. Though both spring from human purposes, houses, unlike fires, never occur in nature when human beings are not at work. Let us refer to the picnicker's fire as an artificial *happening* and to Crusoe's house as an artificial *product*.

Third, Crusoe's house, though an artificial product, is not something wholly artificial. It was made out of natural materials, not out of nothing. It is, therefore, unlike the world itself that, according to the Bible, God created out of nothing. Let us always call things that men make out of natural materials their *productions* rather than their *creations*.

Fourth, we considered human children and the offspring of other animals. Do we ordinarily call them either productions or creations? No, the language we use for describing their coming to be involves such words as "reproduction" and "procreation."

Let us take that fact as significant. The results of biological reproduction or procreation are not like the fire caused by lightning— a *natural event*; nor like the fire built by man—an *artificial happening;* nor like the house that Crusoe erected—an *artificial product;* nor like the world that God created out of nothing.

However, understanding how men build houses will help us to understand how animals reproduce or procreate offspring. Understanding how men make fires happen will help us to understand how fires happen as natural events. Understanding the difference between making fires happen and building houses will help us to understand the difference between fires happening in nature and animals reproducing their kind.

Do not ask now whether understanding all this will also help us to understand how God created the world. That question must wait until we see whether our understanding of the works of nature and of art leads us back to the Bible's story of creation—a story that Aristotle never read.

5

Change and Permanence

Aristotle took a sensible attitude toward the thinkers who preceded him. He said he thought it was wise to pay attention to what they had to say in order to discover which of their opinions were correct and which were incorrect. By sifting the true from the false, some advance might be made.

Two earlier thinkers—Heraclitus and Parmenides—held very extreme views about the world. Heraclitus declared that everything, absolutely everything, was constantly changing. Nothing, absolutely nothing, ever remained the same. One of his followers, Cratylus, even went so far as to say that this made it impossible to use language to communicate, for words are constantly changing their meanings. The only way to communicate is by wiggling your finger.

At the other extreme, Parmenides declared that permanence reigns supreme. Whatever is, is; whatever is not, is not; nothing ever comes into existence or perishes; nothing at all changes, nothing moves. The appearance of change and motion, which Parmenides acknowledged as part of our daily experience, is an illusion. We are being deceived by our senses. In reality, everything always remains the same.

You may wonder how Parmenides could persuade anyone to accept so extreme a view, and one so contrary to our everyday experience. One of his followers, a man named Zeno, tried to invent arguments that would persuade us that when we perceived things moving about, we were being deceived. We were suffering an illusion.

One of these arguments ran somewhat like, this: You want to hit a ball from one end of the tennis court to another. In order to get there, the ball first has to go through half the distance. It has to reach the net. In order to get there, it first has to go through half the distance—at least the service box. In order to get there, it first has to go through half the distance; and so on indefinitely, by a continual halving of the distances that remain. From this, if we followed the direction of Zeno's reasoning, we would be led to the conclusion that the ball could never get started—could never leave your racket.

Aristotle was acquainted with these opinions and arguments. His common sense as well as his common experience told him they were wrong. If words are always changing their meanings, how could Heraclitus and his followers repeatedly say that everything is changing and suppose, as they obviously did, that they were saying the same thing each time, not the opposite? If the motion of the heavenly bodies is an illusion, then so is the change from day to night. If nothing comes into existence or perishes, no one dies, but where are Parmenides and his friend Zeno now?

Heraclitus and Parmenides were wrong, but not all wrong. In fact, each was partly right, and the whole truth, Aristotle thought, consisted in combining two partial truths.

On the one hand, motion and change, coming to be and passing away, occur throughout the world of nature and were occurring long before human beings came on the scene. Far from being full of illusions, our common experience of nature grasps the reality of change. Things are the way they seem to be—changing.

On the other hand, not everything is always

changing in every respect. In every change, there must be something permanent—something that persists or remains the same while becoming different in one respect or another. That tennis ball, for example, which you tried to hit across the court, did move from one place to another, but when it reached your opponent's baseline, it was the same tennis ball that you propelled in that direction. If it had been a different tennis ball, conjured up by a magician standing on the sidelines, it would have been called a foul.

Motion from here to there (which Aristotle called local motion or change of place) is the most obvious of the changes in which something remains the same. The moving thing is the unchanging subject of the change that is local motion. If it was "your tennis ball" when it left your racket, it is still "your tennis ball" when your opponent hits it back—the selfsame, identical ball, not another ball.

While we are talking about local motion, let me mention a distinction that Aristotle makes between two kinds of local motion. When you accidentally drop a tennis ball, it falls to the ground because it is heavy (you and I say because of gravity, which is another word for heavy). You did not throw it down. It fell naturally. That was a natural, not an artificial, motion.

But when you hit the tennis ball with your racket, that is a man-made motion, not a natural one. The force of your stroke overcomes the natural tendency of the ball to fall because of its weight, and this force sends it on a path it would not have followed if you had not propelled it in that direction by your stroke. The same thing is true when we propel a rocket to the moon. That is not a natural motion for a heavy body like a rocket. Without the propelling force we give it, it would not naturally leave the earth's field of gravity.

From tennis balls to rockets, from elevators to cannonballs, there is a wide variety of bodies in local motion that would not be moving as they do were it not for man's interference with nature. Since they are not natural, should we call these motions artificial? That word might be used, for they are motions brought about by men. Aristotle called them violent motions—

violent in the sense that they violate the natural tendency of the bodies in question.

What other changes that occur naturally also occur artificially, or through man's having a hand in them? The heat of the sun ripens a tomato and turns it from green to red. That is not a change in place, but a change in color. It is not a local motion, but the alteration of an attribute of the tomato.

From being green at one time, the tomato has become red at another, just as the tennis ball, from being here at one time, is there at another. What is common to these two changes is time, not space. No change of place occurred in the ripening of the tomato, only a change in quality; but neither change—the change in place and the change in quality—took place without a change in time.

People paint green things red, or red things green—houses, tables, chairs, and so on. The ripening of the tomato is a natural alteration; the painting of things is an artificial alteration of them. The house, table, or chair, which was at one time green, did not become red at another time without human intervention.

In addition to local motion (or change in place) and alteration (or change in quality), there is still a third kind of change that is both natural and artificial. This time let us begin with the artificial form of it.

Take a rubber balloon and blow it up. As you do so, it changes in size as well as in shape. It gets larger, and will continue to do so as you blow air into it. And when you let air out of it, it decreases in size and returns to its original shape.

Left on the table by itself, the balloon would not have increased in size. Blown up, with its end twisted and bound, the balloon will not decrease in size. The change in size, accompanied by a change in shape, is your doing. You have caused two artificial changes to occur at the same time—a change in quality (the alteration of the balloon's shape) and a change in quantity (the increase or decrease in the balloon's size).

Changes in quantity occur naturally as well as artificially. For example, rocks on a seacoast wear away as they are continually battered by waves. They get smaller. The action of waves may also make seacoast caves larger. More familiar experiences of natural increase—in size and weight—occur in the world of living things. Plants and animals grow. Their growth involves many changes, of course, but among them are changes in quantity—increases in size and weight.

Although one aspect of the growth of a living body is certainly an increase or a change in quantity, it has a peculiar characteristic that we do not find in the increase of inanimate bodies. You build a fire and you can make it larger by adding more logs. If more and more logs are available to pile on it, there would appear to be no limit to the size of the fire you can build. If you feed carrots to a rabbit, the rabbit grows in size, but no matter how many carrots you feed the rabbit, there is a limit to the rabbit's increase in size.

You can build smaller or larger pyramids and, given enough stones and human labor, you can make one larger than any pyramid that has ever been built. But no matter what you do in the feeding of animals, you cannot make them grow to be larger than a certain size. You cannot make a house cat the size of a lion or a tiger.

The reverse is also true. The balloon you blew up decreases in size as you let the air out of it, and the decrease can go on to the point where the balloon is completely collapsed. But when animals cease to grow, they may cease to increase in size, but they do not decrease in size to the vanishing point so long as they remain alive.

But animals and plants die. So, too, do balloons burst and cease to be balloons when you blow too much air into them. This brings us to a fourth kind of change—both natural and artificial—that is so different from the other three that Aristotle separates it sharply from the rest.

All the others, as we have seen, take time to happen. Time elapses as bodies move from here to there, alter in color or shape, get larger or smaller. But when the balloon bursts, it ceases to be a balloon instantane-

ously. That change would appear to take no time, certainly no appreciable amount of time. It occurs in an
instant; or perhaps we should say: at one instant the
balloon exists, and at the very next instant it no longer
exists. All we have left are shreds or fragments of rubber, not a balloon we can blow up.

The same is true of the rabbit that dies. In one instant it is alive; at the next, it is no more. All we have
left is the carcass, which, in the course of further time,
will progressively decay and disintegrate.

This special kind of change (which Aristotle refers
to as coming to be and passing away) is special in
other ways than being instantaneous. It is so special
that it raises serious problems for us.

In every change, we have been saying so far,
something remains permanent and unchanging. The
body or thing that changes in place, in color, or in size
remains the same body when it moves from one place
or another, when it alters in color, when it increases in
size. But what remains the same when the balloon
bursts? What remains the same when the rabbit dies?
The decaying, disintegrating carcass is not the rabbit
we fed carrots to. The shreds of rubber are not the balloon we blew up.

Nevertheless, there is something permanent in this
special kind of change. It is easier to see what it is in
the production or destruction of things by men than it
is in the birth and death of plants and animals.

Pieces of wood, nails, and glue do not come together naturally to make a chair. Men make chairs by
putting these materials together in a certain way. They
are the same materials *before* they were put together
and shaped into a chair as they are *after* that happens,
at the instant when the chair comes into existence as
something you can sit on.

You find the chair uncomfortable or you have
other chairs and want a table instead of this one. You
probably cannot reuse all the nails or the glue, but you
can take the chair apart and, using the pieces of wood
and some of the nails, you can build a small table with
most of the same materials. If you had not used glue in

the first place, and if you had been able to extract all the nails in usable form, the materials in the chair that has ceased to be and in the table that has come into being would be identical. They would differ only in respect to how they are put together.

It would, therefore, appear to be the case that in artificial productions and destructions, what persists or remains the same throughout the change is not the thing that was produced and destroyed, but only the materials that a person used in putting it together and the materials that are left when it is taken apart.

Something like that is also the case in the death of the rabbit. Being a living body, the rabbit is, after all, a material thing, just as the chair or table is a material thing. There is matter in its makeup. And that matter remains, not in the same form, of course, but nevertheless it remains, when the rabbit breaks up—dies, decays, disintegrates. And just as the inorganic materials of a chair may enter into the composition of a table, so the organic materials of a rabbit may enter into the composition of another living thing.

The rabbit may have been killed by a jackal and devoured for nourishment. To the extent that the jackal is able to assimilate what it eats, the organic materials of the rabbit enter into the bone, flesh, and muscle of the jackal.

Modern science has a name for what is going on here—a name that Aristotle did not use. We call it the conservation of matter. However it is referred to, the point is that something persists in the special kind of change that is coming to be and passing away. That something, in the case of artificial things such as tables and chairs, consists of the materials out of which they are made.

In man-made productions, we can usually identify what these materials are—these particular pieces of wood, these particular nails. It is not always as easy to identify the particular unit or units of matter that persist when one animal eats another or when living things die. But there can be no doubt that in all instances of coming to be and passing away, both natural and artificial, either matter itself or materials of a certain kind undergo transformation.

What is meant by "matter itself" as contrasted with "materials of a certain kind"? Human beings, in making or destroying artificial things, never work with matter itself, but only with materials of a certain kind. Does nature, unlike man, work with matter itself? If so, then that which persists or remains the subject of change in artificial production and destruction is not the same as that which persists or remains the subject of change in natural coming to be and passing away.

Similar, but not the same. The transformation of identifiable materials in human production and destruction is only like but not identical with the transformation of matter in natural coming to be and passing away. Nevertheless, the similarity or likeness may help us to understand what happens when, in nature, things come to be and pass away. We will look into this more closely in the following chapters.

6

The Four Causes

The "four causes" are the answers that Aristotle gives to four questions that can and should be asked about the changes with which we are acquainted in our common experience. They are common-sense questions, and so are the answers. Let us begin by considering them as they apply to changes brought about by human beings, especially the things they produce or make. That will help us to consider the four causes as they operate in the workings of nature.

The first question about any human production is: What is it going to be made of? If you asked this question of a shoemaker at work, the answer would be "leather." If you asked it of a jeweler, fashioning bracelets or rings out of precious metals, the answer might be "gold" or "silver." If you asked it of a gunsmith producing a rifle, the answer would probably be "wood and steel" The kind of material named in each case, on which the craftsman works and out of which he is producing a particular product, is the *material* cause of the production. It is one of four indispensable factors—factors without which the production would not and could not occur.

The second question is: Who made it? That

would appear to be the easiest question of all, at least when we are dealing with human productions. It may not be so easy when we come to the changes that take place in nature and to the things produced by nature rather than by men. So far as human productions are concerned, the question has already been answered in what was said in answer to the first question: the shoemaker is the maker of the shoe, the jeweler of the bracelets or rings, the gunsmith of the gun. The maker in each case is the *efficient* cause of the production.

The third question is: What is it that is being made? On the face of it, that question is so easy that it may make you impatient to have to consider it. It is obvious, you may say, that what is being made by the shoemaker is a shoe, by the jeweler a ring, and so on. But when I tell you that Aristotle called the answer to this question the *formal* cause of the change or production, you may be puzzled by the introduction of that word "formal," though it is, as you will soon see, the precise word to pair with "material," the first of the four causes. I will return to the explanation of "formal" after we have considered the last of the four causes.

The fourth question is: What is it being made for? What purpose is it intended to fulfill? What objective or use did the maker have in mind as the end to serve? In its simplest form, the question is: Why is it being made? And the answer, with regard to the productions we have been talking about, comes quickly. We all know what shoes and rings and guns are for— what function they perform or what purpose they serve.

This fourth factor in human productions Aristotle called the *final* cause, calling it that because the factor being referred to is an *end* in view. When you or I make anything, the end we have in mind is something that we achieve last or finally. We must finish making it before we can put it to use for the purpose we had in mind.

I said earlier that the four causes are indispensable factors that must be present and operative whenever men produce anything. To call them indispensable is to say that, taken together, they are that without which the production could not have taken place. Each of the four factors, taken by itself, is necessary, but none by itself is sufficient.

All four must be present together and operate in relation to one another in a certain way. The workman must have material to work on and must actually work on it. By doing so, he must transform it into something that the materials in hand can be made to become. And what has been made must be of some use to the person making it. In other words, he must have had a reason for making it, for without that, he would probably not have expended the effort to make it.

You may question the last of these statements. You may wonder whether the final cause—the reason for making something—must always be present and operating. Isn't it possible for someone to produce something without having a reason for doing so—without having in mind, in advance, a deliberate purpose that he wishes to serve?

That question is not easy to answer with certainty, though you must admit that, for the most part, human beings do make the effort to produce things because they need or want the things they are engaged in producing. Yet they may also, on occasion, fiddle around with materials and, as a result, produce something unexpected—aimlessly or, shall we say, playfully.

When this happens, there would appear to be no final cause, no end result being aimed at. A purpose for the object produced, a function for it to perform, may be thought up after the production is completed, but the producer of it did not have it in mind in advance. It could, therefore, hardly have been an indispensable factor, or a cause, of what occurred.

When we turn from human productions to the workings of nature, the question about the presence and operation of final causes becomes more insistent. We cannot avoid facing it squarely, for we should certainly be uneasy about saying that nature has this or that in mind as the end result that it aims at. Perhaps, when I am able to explain why Aristotle calls the third of the four causes the *formal* cause, I will also be able to answer the question about the operation of final causes in the workings of nature.

Before I do so, let me summarize the four causes by describing them in the simplest terms possible. Because these statements about the four causes are so very simple, they may also be difficult to understand. We must pay close attention to the key words that are *italicized* in each statement.

1. Material cause: that *out of which* something is made.
2. Efficient cause: that *by which* something is made.
3. Formal cause: that *into which* something is made.
4. Final cause: that *for the sake of which* something is made.

What do we mean when we say "that *into which* something is made"? The leather out of which the shoe was made by the shoemaker was not a shoe before the shoemaker went to work on it. It became a shoe or got turned into a shoe by the work he did, which transformed it from being merely a piece of leather into being a shoe made out of leather. That, which at an earlier time was leather not having the form of a shoe, is now at a later time leather formed into a shoe. That is why Aristotle says that "shoeness" is the formal cause in the production of shoes.

The introduction of that word "shoeness" will help us to avoid the worst error we can make in dealing with formal causes. We might be tempted, very naturally, to think of the form of a thing as its shape—something we are able to sketch on a piece of paper. But shoes come in a wide variety of shapes, as well as colors and sizes. If you stood in front of a shoestore window with sketch pad in hand, you would find it very difficult or impossible to draw what is common to the various shapes of the shoes in the window.

You can think of what is common to them, but you cannot draw it. When you do have an idea of what is common to all shoes, of every shape, size, and color, then you have grasped the form that Aristotle calls *shoeness*. Without there being such a form, shoes could never be made; the raw materials out of which shoes are made could never be transformed into shoes.

Please notice that word "transform." It contains the word "form." When you transform raw materials into something that they are not—leather into shoes, gold into bracelets, and so on—you are giving them a form that they did not previously have. A shoemaker, by working on raw materials, transforms them into something they can become but which, before he worked on them, they were not.

We can get further away from the mistake of thinking that the formal cause is the shape a thing takes by considering other kinds of change that we discussed before—changes other than the production of things such as shoes, rings, and guns.

The tennis ball you set in motion moves from your racket across the court to your opponent's baseline. You are the efficient cause of that motion, propelling the ball by the force of your stroke. The ball is the material cause—that which is being acted on. But what is the formal cause? It must be some place other than the place from which the ball started out when you hit it. Let us suppose that the ball lands on the other side of the net, is missed by your opponent, and comes to rest against the back fence. The place where it comes to rest is the formal cause of the particular motion that ended there. From having been *here,* on your side of the net, its position or place has been transformed into being *over there,* against the back fence.

The green chair that you paint red is similarly transformed in color. So, too, the balloon you blew up; it is transformed in size. *Redness* is the formal cause of the change you brought about by painting the chair, just as *overthereness* is the formal cause of the change you brought about by hitting the tennis ball. In each of these changes, you are the efficient cause. In one of them, the green chair is the material cause, that which you acted on in painting it red. In the other, the collapsed balloon is the material cause, that which you acted on when you blew it up.

The three kinds of change just considered also occur naturally, without man entering the picture as efficient cause. When we examine their natural occurrence, identifying the four causes becomes more difficult, and some new problems arise. However, what has already been said about humanly caused changes will be of some help to us.

Sunshine ripens the tomato and turns it from green to red. The rays of the sun are the efficient cause of this alteration, and the tomato itself, the subject undergoing the change, is the material cause of it. Here, as in a person's painting a green chair red, redness is the formal cause. From having been green in color, that is what the tomato becomes. But here there is no final cause distinct from the formal cause just named.

The person who painted the green chair red may have done so for the sake of having it match a set of chairs in a certain room. The purpose or end the individual had in mind was distinct from the redness that was the formal cause in the transformation of the chair's color. But we would hardly say that the sun, in shining on the tomato, wished to make it red as a sign that it had at last become edible. The end result of the tomato's ripening, so far as its surface color is concerned, consists in its being red. Its being red is both the formal and the final cause of the change.

Much of the same can be said about the rock that wears away under the battering of the waves, becoming smaller in size as a result of that process. This process may go on for a long time, but at any given moment, the size of the rock at that time is both the formal and the final cause of the change—the decrease in size that has occurred so far.

The account just given of a natural alteration in color and a natural decrease in size applies as well to a natural change of place. The tennis ball that is accidentally dropped falls to the ground and eventually comes to rest there. That local motion comes to an end at the place where the ball comes to rest, and that place is the formal as well as the final cause of the motion.

If, in this case, one were to talk about the efficient

cause, the force of gravity would probably be named—an answer that most of us learned in school, but that would have puzzled Aristotle. That fact does not affect our understanding of the difference between an efficient cause, on the one hand, and material, final, and formal causes, on the other. However it is named or designated, it is always that which, in any process of change, acts upon a changeable subject or exerts an influence upon it that results in that changeable subject's becoming different in a certain respect—red, from having been green; smaller, from having been larger; there, from having been here.

Let us consider one other kind of change—the growth of a living thing that, though it involves increase in size, involves much more than this. Aristotle uses the familiar example of the acorn that falls to the ground from an oak, takes root there, is nurtured by sunshine, rain, and nutrients in the soil, and eventually develops into another full-grown oak tree.

The acorn, he tells us, is an oak in the process of becoming. What it is to be oak is both the final and the formal cause of the acorn's turning into an oak. The form that the acorn assumes when, through growth, it reaches its full development is the end that the acorn was destined to reach simply by virtue of its being an acorn.

If, instead of being an acorn, the seedling had been a kernel taken from an ear of corn, our planting it and nurturing it would have resulted in a different end product—a stalk of corn with ears on it. According to Aristotle, the end that is to be achieved and the form that is to be developed in the process of growth are somehow present at the very beginning—in the seed that, with proper nurturing, grows into the fully developed plant.

They are not present actually, he would acknowledge, for then the acorn would already be an oak, and the kernel a stalk of corn. But they are present potentially, which is simply the opposite of their being present actually. It is the difference between the potentiality that is present in the acorn, on the one hand, and the potentiality that is present in the corn kernel, on the other, which causes the one seed to develop in one way and the other seed to develop in another.

Today we have a different way of saying the same thing. Aristotle said that the "entelechy" of one seed differed from the "entelechy" of the other. All he meant by that Greek word was that each seed had in it a potentiality that destined it to reach, through growth and development, a different final form or end result. We say, when we use the language of modern science, that the genetic code in one seed gives it a set of directions for growth and development that is different from the set of directions given by the genetic code in the other seed.

We think of the genetic code as programming a living thing's growth and development from the very moment when that process starts. Aristotle thought of a living thing's inherent potentialities as guiding and controlling what it becomes in its process of growth and development. Up to a certain point, the two descriptions of what happens are almost interchangeable. The observable facts to be accounted for remain the same. Acorns never turn into cornstalks.

That this is so must be because there is something initially different in the matter that constitutes the acorn, on the one hand, and in the matter that constitutes the kernel of table corn, on the other. Calling what is there genes that program growth and development or calling them potentialities that guide and control growth and development does not make much difference to our understanding of what is going on. But, as most of us know, it does make a difference to what human beings can do to interfere with natural processes.

Our scientific knowledge of DNA (an abbreviation for a term in biochemistry) enables us to experiment with the genetic code of an organism and, perhaps, to make significant changes in the directions it gives. Aristotle's philosophical understanding of the role that potentialities play did not enable him, nor does it enable us, to interfere in the slightest way with the workings of nature.

I shall have more to say in the next chapter about potentialities and actualities, and also about matter and form, as fundamental factors in changes of all sorts, both natural and artificial. These four factors, although not identical with the four causes, are closely related to them.

To whet your appetite for what is coming next, let me ask you to consider again one more change that has already been mentioned—the special kind of change that Aristotle called coming to be and passing away. As an example of that special kind of change, I am going to take an occurrence that is most familiar to us in our everyday life.

We sit down to dinner and, in the course of it, we eat a piece of fruit. The apple on our plate, when taken from the tree, had finished growing. But it is still a living thing, with seeds in it that can be planted to sprout more apple trees. It shows no signs of decay or rotting. We eat it, all but the core. What has become of the apple?

We have not only eaten it, chewed it up, digested it, but we also have drawn some nourishment from it, which means that it has somehow become part of us. Before we started eating it, the organic matter of that piece of fruit had the form of an apple. After we finished eating, digesting, and drawing nourishment from it, the matter, which once had the form of an apple, has somehow become fused or merged with your own matter, which has the form of a human being.

The apple has not become a human being. Rather, it would appear, matter itself has been transformed, from having the form of an apple to having the form of a human being. It ceased to be apple matter and became human matter.

What is meant by "matter itself" as opposed to "apple matter" and "human matter"? Can we say that matter itself is that which remains the permanent underlying subject of change in this remarkable kind of change that happens every day when we eat the food that nourishes us?

I hope I can throw some light on these "matters" in the next chapter.

7

To Be and Not To Be

We ordinarily think of the birth of a living organism as the coming into being of something that did not
exist before. And we often refer to the death of a person as his or her passing away.

In Aristotle's thought about the changes that occur in the world of nature and the changes that human
beings bring about by their effort, the special kind of
change that he calls coming to be and passing away is
distinguished from all other kinds of change, such as
change of place, alteration in quality, and increase or
decrease in quantity.

This special kind of change in nature is more difficult to understand than other kinds of change. Why?
To find out, let us begin with what is easier to understand—the production or destruction of things by human beings.

When people move things from one place to another, when they alter or enlarge them, the individual
thing that they move, alter, or enlarge remains the selfsame thing. It changes only with respect to its attributes—its place, its color, its size. It not only remains
the same kind of thing that it was before it changed;

45

after it has been changed, it also persists as this one, unique, individual thing.

The enduring sameness or permanence of the individual thing that undergoes these changes is clear to us from the fact that its identity can be named in the same way before and after the change occurs: *this* ball, *that* chair. It is not another ball or another chair, but this one or that one.

When someone takes raw materials, such as pieces of wood, and transforms those raw materials into a chair, an artificial thing—something that did not exist before—comes into existence. What before were several pieces of wood have now become this particular chair. Pieces of wood becoming a chair is certainly not the same as this green chair becoming red. The reason is that when the chair has come into being, the several separate pieces of wood no longer remain, at least not as several separate pieces of wood, though this chair remains precisely this chair when it changes in color.

Before we go from artificial production to natural generation (which is just another name for the process of coming to be), it will be helpful to us if we look a little more closely at what is happening in the easier-to-understand process of artificial production. The help will come from getting some grasp of the meaning of four words that were used in the preceding chapter. They are "matter," "form," "potentiality," and "actuality." Though what they mean can be understood in the light of common experience and in common-sense terms, the words themselves are not words we use frequently in everyday speech.

Pieces of wood that are not a chair become pieces of wood that are a chair. When the pieces of wood are not a chair, their not being a chair is a lack of chairness on their part. They lack—they are deprived of—the form of a chair. Let's use the word "privation" for this lack of a certain form.

There is more in these pieces of wood than the privation of chairness. If that was all there was to it, these pieces of wood could never be made into a chair. In addition to lacking chairness, these pieces of wood must also have the capacity to acquire chairness. Their capacity is inseparably connected with their privation, for if these pieces of wood did not lack the form of a chair, they would not have the capacity for acquiring that form, since not lacking it, they would already have it. Only when certain materials, such as pieces of wood, lack a certain form can they have the capacity for acquiring it.

Let us call that capacity a potentiality of the materials in question. Another word for *potentiality* is "can be." It makes a great deal of difference whether you say that something *is* a chair or *can be* a chair. These pieces of wood *are not* a chair, but they *can be* a chair. As I said a moment ago, if they were a chair, they could not become a chair.

However, it is not true to say that when certain materials lack a certain form, they always have the potentiality for acquiring it. For example, water and air lack the form of a chair, but unlike wood, water and air are materials that do not have the potentiality for acquiring the form of a chair. Although the potentiality for acquiring a certain form is never present in the materials unless that form is absent, the mere absence of the form—the lack or privation of it—does not necessarily mean that the materials have the potentiality for acquiring it. Men can make chairs out of wood, but not out of air or water.

When the pieces of wood that lack the form of a chair and also have the potentiality for acquiring that form take on that form as a result of a carpenter's skill and effort, we say that the pieces of wood that were potentially a chair have now actually become a chair. Throughout the whole process of becoming, until the very moment when the chair is finally finished, the pieces of wood, undergoing transformation, were still only potentially a chair. Not until their transformation has been completed do they actually have the form of a chair.

When the pieces of wood are actually a chair, their potentiality for becoming a chair has been *actualized;* and so, of course, it no longer remains as a potentiality. The form the pieces of wood have acquired is the actuality that removes the potentiality that accompanied the lack of that form in the wood but did not accompany the lack of it in water or air.

We can now see how these four important words—matter, form, potentiality, and actuality—are related. Matter may have or lack a certain form. Lacking it, matter may also have the capacity for acquiring it, which is its potentiality for having that form. But it does not always have such a potentiality when it lacks a certain form, as we saw in the case of water and air as compared with wood. When it acquires the form for which it has a potentiality, that potentiality has been actualized. Having the acquired form has transformed the matter from being a potential chair into being an actual chair.

I have been using the words "matter" and "materials" interchangeably. But when we are referring to wood, on the one hand, and water, on the other, we are speaking of different kinds of matter. Wood is not just matter, it is a certain kind of matter—matter having the form of wood, which is different from matter having the form of water.

One kind of matter, wood, provides human beings with materials out of which they can make chairs; another kind, water, does not. The form the matter has, which makes it a certain kind of matter (wood), also gives it a certain potentiality (for becoming a chair). Matter in the form of water does not have that potentiality.

When we understand this simple point, a simple step of reasoning enables us to grasp another important point.

Wood can become a chair, but it cannot become an electric light bulb; water can become a fountain, but it cannot become a chair.

Matter having a certain form has a limited potentiality for acquiring other forms. This is true of every kind of matter, all the different kinds of materials that people can work on to produce things—chairs, electric light bulbs, and fountains.

Now suppose there was matter totally deprived of form—utterly formless matter. It would not actually be any kind of matter. But it would also be potentially every kind of matter; since, lacking all forms, it would have the capacity to acquire any form. It would have an unlimited potentiality for forms.

You would be quite right if, thinking about this, you were to say: "Hold on, matter without any form might have an unlimited potentiality, an unlimited capacity, for acquiring forms, but lacking all forms, it would be actually nothing. What is actually nothing does not exist. Hence to talk about formless matter is to talk about something that cannot exist." Why, then, you may ask, did I bother to mention it in the first place? What's the point in thinking about it?

Aristotle would say that, looked at in one way, you are right in thinking that pure matter, formless matter, is not actually anything or, in other words, is nothing. You are, therefore, also right in thinking that formless matter does not exist. But Aristotle would add that, although formless matter is actually nothing, it is also potentially everything. It is potentially every possible kind of thing that can be.

Still, you persist in asking, if formless matter does not exist and cannot exist, what is the point in mentioning it or thinking about it? Aristotle's answer is that there would be no need to mention it or think about it if we confined ourselves to trying to understand artificial productions and destructions—the making and unmaking of such things as chairs. But the birth and death of animals are not so easy to understand.

Let's take an animal's death first. Our pet rabbit dies—decays, disintegrates, and eventually disappears. The matter that had the form of a rabbit no longer has that form. It now has acquired another form, as would happen if the rabbit were killed and devoured by a wolf. When this happens, matter that was the matter of one kind of thing (rabbit) has now become the matter of another kind of thing (wolf).

If you think about this for a moment, you will see that what has occurred here is different from what occurred when wood, which is a certain kind of matter, becomes a chair. Becoming a chair, it does not cease to be wood. It does not cease to be matter of a certain kind. A certain kind of matter has persisted throughout this change. It can be identified as the subject of the change. These pieces of wood that at one time were not actually a chair have now become actually a chair.

But in the transformation that occurred when the wolf killed and devoured the rabbit, a certain kind of matter did not persist throughout the change. The matter of a certain kind of thing (matter having the form of a rabbit) became the matter of another kind of thing (matter having the form of a wolf). The only identifiable subject of this change is matter—not matter of a certain kind, since matter of *a particular kind* does not persist throughout the change.

Let us now turn from death to birth. That pet rabbit of yours came into being as a result of sexual reproduction. Aristotle was as well acquainted with the facts of life as you and I are. The process that results in the birth of a living rabbit began when an ovum of a female rabbit was fertilized by the sperm of a male rabbit.

From the moment of fertilization, a new organism has begun to develop, though while it is still being carried in the female rabbit's uterus, it is not a separate living thing. The birth of the rabbit is just a phase in the rabbit's process of development. It has been developing within the mother rabbit before being born, and it goes on developing after it is born until it reaches full growth.

Birth is nothing but the separation of one living body from another—the baby rabbit from the mother rabbit. And that separation is a local motion, a movement of the baby rabbit from being in one place to being in another—from being inside the mother rabbit to being outside the mother rabbit.

Let us now go back to the beginning of the baby rabbit—the moment when it first came to be. Before that moment, there was the female rabbit's ovum and the male rabbit's sperm. Neither that ovum nor the sperm was actually a rabbit, though both together had the potentiality for becoming a rabbit. The actualization of that potentiality took place at the moment of fertilization, when the matter of the sperm was merged or fused with the matter of ovum.

Do the matter of the ovum and the matter of the sperm in separation from each other stand in the same relation to the matter of the baby rabbit after fertilization occurs, as the matter of the rabbit stands to the matter of the wolf after the rabbit has been killed and devoured by the wolf? If so, then something like what Aristotle had in mind when he asked us to think about formless matter is the subject of change in the coming to be and passing away of living organisms. It is that which we identify as persisting or enduring in this special kind of change.

This is as near as I can come to explaining why Aristotle thought it necessary to mention formless matter. You may think that he went too far—that natural generation can be accounted for in the same way as artificial production. If you do think so, let me ask you to consider one more example.

The example is one that Aristotle himself considered. He said that "nature proceeds little by little from things lifeless to living things in such a way that it is impossible to determine the exact line of demarcation." He was quite capable of imaginging the line between the nonliving and the living being crossed when the first living organism on earth emerged from nonliving matter. In that coming to be of the first living organisms, can we identify the matter that is the subject of this remarkable change as being matter of a certain kind? Does it remain the same kind of matter both before and after the first living organisms came into being?

You may not want to go so far as to call it formless matter. But, on the other hand, you may find it difficult to identify it as matter of a certain kind, which would mean that it had and retained a certain form. If this is your state of mind, then you understand why Aristotle thought natural generation more difficult to explain than artificial production; and you also understand why he thought it necessary to mention and ask you to think about pure or formless matter, which, of course, does not exist.

8

Productive Ideas and
Know-How

The individual who first took wood and made it into a chair—or a bed or a house—must have had some idea of what he was going to make or build before setting to work. Such an individual had to understand the form that the pieces of wood would have to acquire in order to become a chair. He could not get that idea from an experience with chairs because no chairs existed before he made this one. Perhaps, we may guess, he got it from experiences with rock formations that provided his body with support for sitting down. The first chair was thus an imitation of something its inventor had found in nature, as the first house was, perhaps, an imitation of natural cave formations that provided shelter.

Wherever or however the first chairmaker got the idea of a chair, the idea itself was not enough. As we observed in an earlier chapter, the form of a chair—chairness—is common to chairs of every size, shape, and configuration of parts. If all that the first carpenter had in his mind was an idea of chairs in general, he could not have produced an individual chair, particular in every respect in which one individual chair can differ from others. In order to transform the wood materials he worked on, by giving those materials the form of a chair, he also had to have some idea of the particular chair he was about to produce.

Productive thinking involves having what we may be tempted to call creative ideas. Since no Greek equivalent of the word "creative" was in Aristotle's vocabulary, we should resist that temptation, and speak instead of productive ideas. Productive ideas are based on some understanding of the forms that matter can take, supplemented by imaginative thinking about such details as sizes, shapes, and configurations. Without a productive idea in this full sense, the craftsman cannot transform raw materials into this individual thing—be it a chair, a bed, a house, or anything else that can be made out of materials provided by nature.

There are two ways in which a productive idea can be expressed. The first chairmaker or housebuilder probably did not draw up a plan or blueprint of the thing he was about to produce. With a productive idea in mind, he just produced it. The materialization of that idea—its embodiment in matter—expressed the productive idea he had. If you had asked him what idea he had in mind before he made the chair or built the house, he might not have been able to tell you in so many words. But once he had brought the chair or house into existence, he could have pointed to it and said, "There, that is what I had in mind."

Much later in the history of mankind, craftsmen of all sorts became able to draw up plans for the making of things. They became able to express their productive ideas before actually materializing them by transforming matter. But even at later stages in the history of human productivity, craftsmen do not always proceed to work by first putting their productive ideas down on paper in some fashion. They still sometimes hold the idea in their mind and let it guide them in every step of the work until the finished product comes into existence and expresses the idea they had in the first place.

This distinction between two ways in which productive ideas can be expressed calls our attention to two phases in the making of things, phases that can be separated. One individual can have the idea of a particular house to be built and can draw up the plans for the building of that house. Another individual, or other individuals, can execute or carry out that plan. Nowadays we differentiate between these different contributors to the making of a house by calling one an architect and the other a builder (or, if the builder employs other persons to engage in building the house, we call the builder a contractor).

The individual who draws up the plans in the first place is the one who has the productive idea. Those who execute the plans must have know-how. In the making of anything, whether it be a chair or a house, productive ideas are not enough. To carry them out, it is necessary to know how to deal with the raw materials in such a way that their potentiality for becoming a chair or a house is actualized. Unless that end result is reached, the productive idea will not be expressed in matter. It will not be materialized.

Of course, one and the same individual may have both the productive idea and the know-how needed for making a chair or a house. The only thing we must remember is that productive ideas and know-how are distinct factors in the making of things. What enters into the craftsman's know-how?

First of all, he must know how to choose the appropriate raw materials for making the kind of thing he has in mind, with whatever tools he has at his disposal, or with none at all, but only his bare hands. If, for example, his only tools are a hammer and saw, he cannot make a chair out of iron or steel or a house out of stones. And it should go without saying that, regardless of what tools are available, the artisan cannot make a chair or a house out of air or water.

Beyond knowing how to choose the appropriate materials to work on with the tools at his disposal, the craftsman must also know how to use those tools efficiently and how to proceed, step by step, in the construction of the thing he wishes to make. In the building of a house, laying the foundation precedes getting the frame up, as that precedes putting the roof on.

The mind, the hands, and the tools of the craftsman, taken all together, are the efficient cause of the thing that is produced. They act upon the raw materials to actualize the potentialities that such materials have for being transformed into the product that the maker had in mind.

Of these three factors (which together constitute the efficient cause), the mind is the principal factor. It is the maker's mind that has the productive idea and the know-how, without which neither hands nor tools could ever make anything. The maker's hands and his tools are merely the instruments his mind uses to put his productive idea and his know-how into the actions required to act on the raw materials and actualize their potentialities.

The human mind is the principal factor in human production. Everything else is instrumental.

To know how to make something is to have skill. Even in the simplest performances, which we sometimes call unskilled labor, there is some know-how and, therefore, some skill. From the simplest to the most complex activities in which human beings engage— from the building of toy models by children to the building of bridges, dams, and schools—the levels of know-how are the levels of skill.

Another English word for "skill" is the word "technique." The person who has the know-how required for making something has the technique for making it. I mention this because the English word "technique" comes from the Greek word *technikos*, which Aristotle used in talking about the acquired ability that some men may have and others may not have for making things. The combining form *techno-* which means art or skill, comes from the Greek *techné*. In Latin, this becomes *ars* and in English *art*. An artist is a person who has the technique, skill, or know-how for making things. We would call such persons creative artists if, in addition to having the know-how, they also have the productive idea that is the indispensable primary source from which comes the thing to be made.

We sometimes use the word "art" for the things produced by an artist. We use the word as short for "works of art." But since works of art cannot be produced unless someone has acquired the know-how to produce them, art in the sense of know-how must first exist in a human being before it can make itself evident in a work of art.

Although you would readily refer to cooks, dressmakers, carpenters, or shoemakers as artists or craftsmen because you recognized that they had the skill or know-how for making this or that, you would probably not refer to farmers, physicians, or teachers as artists. Aristotle, however, recognized their possession of a certain skill or know-how that would justify calling them artists. But he also pointed out how different their art is from the art of cooks, carpenters, and shoemakers.

The latter produce things—cakes, chairs, and shoes—that would never come into existence without human productive ideas, know-how, and effort. Nature does not produce such things. They are always works of art. But nature, without human know-how and effort, does produce fruits and grains. Why, then, should we refer to farmers, who raise such things as apples or corn, as artists? What have they produced?

By themselves, nothing. Farmers have merely helped nature to produce the apples and the corn that nature would have produced anyway. They have the skill or know-how to cooperate with nature in the production of fruit or grain; and, by so doing, they may be able to obtain a better supply of nature's products than would have fallen to their hands if they had not cooperated with nature in producing them.

As farmers, having the know-how or skills that belong to agriculture, cooperate with nature in the production of fruits, grains, and vegetables, so physicians, having the know-how or skills that belong to medicine, cooperate with nature in preserving or restoring the health of a living organism. Since health, like apples and corn, is something that would exist even if there were no physicians, physicians, as well as farmers, are merely cooperative artists, not productive ones like the shoemakers and the carpenters.

So, too, are teachers. Human beings can acquire knowledge without the aid of teachers, just as apples and corn grow without the aid of farmers. But teachers can help human beings acquire knowledge, just as farmers can help apples and corn to grow in desired qualities and quantities. Teaching, like farming and healing, is a cooperative, not a productive art.

The productive arts differ in many ways. Human making turns out a wide variety of products—from chairs, shoes, and houses to paintings, statues, poems, and songs. Paintings and statues are like shoes and chairs in that they are made of materials that the maker somehow transforms. Also, like shoes and chairs, paintings and statues exist at a given place and at a given time.

On the other hand, a piece of music—a song that is sung over and over again—does not exist just at one place and at one time. It can be sung at many different places and at many different times. In addition, it takes time to sing a song or play a piece of music, as it takes time to recite a poem or tell a story. The song and the story have a beginning, a middle, and an end in a sequence of times, which is not true of a statue or a painting.

There is one further difference between a song or a story and a painting or a statue. Stories can be written down in words; songs can be written down in musical notations. The words of speech and the notations of music are symbols that can be read. The person who is able to read them can get the story that is being told by them, sing the song or hear it. But the painting and the statue must be seen directly. To enjoy the work of a painter or sculptor, you must go to the material product that he has made.

Though the painting or the statue is a material product like the shoe or the chair, it is also something to be enjoyed, like the story or the song, not something to be used, like the shoe or the chair. Of course, it is possible to use a painting to cover a spot on the wall, as it is possible to enjoy a chair by looking at it instead of sitting down on it.

Nevertheless, using and enjoying are different ways that men approach works of art. They use them when they employ them to serve some purpose. They enjoy them when they are satisfied with the pleasure they get from perceiving them in one way or another—by seeing, hearing, or reading.

The pleasure we get when we enjoy a work of art has something to do with our calling the thing we enjoy *beautiful*. But that is not all there is to it. It is also possible to call a chair, a table, or a house beautiful simply because it is well made. Its being well made is one factor that enters into the beauty of a human product, whether it is a chair or a statue. The pleasure we get from beholding it is another factor.

Aristotle's suggestion that these two factors are related appears to make good sense. The pleasure we get from looking at the statue or the house, or listening to the story or the song, is somehow connected with its being well made. A poorly made statue, a poorly constructed house, a poorly told story would not give us as much pleasure.

We all know the difference between a piece of clothing made by a skilled tailor, or a soup made by a skilled cook, and shirts or soups made by persons with very little skill. The well-made shirt and the well-made soup are more enjoyable—give us more pleasure—than poorly made ones.

In addition, those who have the art of cooking or tailoring have the know-how by which they can judge whether a shirt or a soup is well made. We would expect skilled cooks or tailors to agree in their judgments. We would be very surprised if one skilled cook thought a soup was well made and another, having equal skill, thought it was poorly made.

We would not be so surprised if we found that, of two persons looking at a painting that skilled artists agreed was well made, one liked it and the other didn't. We do not expect individuals to enjoy the same things or enjoy them to the same extent. What gives one person pleasure may not give pleasure to another.

Just as one person may have more skill or know-how than another, so one person may have better taste than another. It would be wiser to ask a skilled person whether a certain work of art was well made than to ask that question of a person who did not know anything about how such things should be made. So it might be wiser to ask a person who had better taste about the enjoyability of a work of art. We would expect a person of better taste to like a work of art that was better—not only better made but more enjoyable.

The question whether we should all be able to agree, or whether we should all be expected to agree, about the beauty of a work of art has never been satisfactorily answered. There are some reasons for answering it by saying yes, and some reasons for answering it by saying no. If all there were to the beauty of a work of art consisted in its being well made, the question would be easier to answer. We expect those who have the know-how needed to produce a work of that sort to be able to agree that it is well made or poorly made.

Where does this all important know-how come from? How does the person of skill acquire it?

There are two answers. In the earlier stages of human production, the know-how needed was based on common-sense knowledge of nature—knowledge about the raw materials that nature provided the human producer to work on and knowledge about the use of the tools to be worked with.

In later stages, and especially in modern times, the know-how needed has been based on scientific knowledge of nature, and it now consists of what we have come to call the technology that scientific knowledge gives us. "Technology" is just another name for scientific know-how as compared with common-sense know-how.

Does Aristotle's uncommon common sense give us any useful know-how? Does philosophical thought—the understanding of natural processes that we have been considering in the preceding chapters—help us to produce things?

No, it does not. Scientific knowledge can be applied productively. Scientific knowledge, through technology, gives us the skill and power to produce things. But the philosophical reflection or understanding that improves our common-sense grasp of the physical world in which we live gives us neither the skill nor the power to produce anything.

Remember, for example, something said in an earlier chapter. Aristotle's philosophical understanding of why acorns develop into oaks and kernels of corn develop into stalks of corn does not enable us to interfere with these natural processes in any way. But our scientific knowledge about DNA and the genetic code does enable us to alter the pattern of development by splicing the genes.

Is philosophy totally useless, then, as compared with science? Yes, it is, if we confine ourselves to the use of knowledge or understanding for the sake of producing things. Philosophy bakes no cakes and builds no bridges.

But there is a use of knowledge or understanding other than the use we put it to when we engage in the production of things. Knowledge and understanding can be used to direct our lives and manage our societies so that they are better rather than worse lives and better rather than worse societies.

That is a practical rather than a productive use of knowledge and understanding—a use for the sake of doing rather than a use for the sake of making.

In that dimension of human life, philosophy is highly useful—more useful than science.

PART III

MAN THE DOER

9

Thinking about
Ends and Means

I do not have an automobile and I want one. The automobile I want costs more money than I have available. It is necessary for me to get the money needed to buy the car. There appear to be a number of ways in which I can get what is needed without violating the law. For example, I can save it, by not spending what money I have on something else; or I can try to earn additional money; or I can borrow it.

In this example—there might have been countless others of the same sort—getting the automobile is the end in view. Getting the money needed to buy the car is a means to that end; it is also itself an end to which there are, as we have seen, a number of means.

How do I choose among them? One may be easier than the others; going one way may get me my goal more quickly than going the other ways. Of the several means, each serving to attain the end in view, one would normally choose the means that seems better by virtue of being easier, quicker, more likely to succeed, and so on.

When we act this way, we act purposefully. To say that we have a purpose in what we do is to say that we are acting for some goal that we have in mind.

Sometimes we act aimlessly—like a boat just drifting on the current with no one at the wheel to steer it. When we act in that way, we are also acting thoughtlessly. We have nothing in mind that guides our acting in one direction or another. To act aimlessly requires no thinking on our part.

For the most part, however, we act purposefully, and then we cannot act without thinking first. We have to think about the goal we are aiming at—the end we are trying to achieve. We have to think about the various means that we can use to achieve it. We have to think about which is the better of alternative means and why one is better than another. And if the particular means that we choose to employ is a means we cannot use without doing something else first in order to lay our hands on it, then it is itself an end, and we must think about the means to achieving it.

Thinking of the sort I have just described is practical thinking. It is thinking about ends and means—thinking about the goal you wish to reach and thinking about what must be done to get there. It is the kind of thinking that is necessary for purposeful action.

Productive thinking, as we have seen, is thinking about things to be made. Practical thinking, in contrast, is thinking about what is to be done. To think well for the sake of making something, you have to have what we called productive ideas and know-how. To think well for the sake of getting somewhere by what you do, you have to have an idea of a goal to be reached and ideas about ways of reaching it. And you also have to think about the reasons why one way of pursuing your goal is better than another.

Productive thinking, or thinking in order to produce something, does not actually produce it. Such thinking may lead to actual production, but production does not actually begin until the producer goes to work and acts on the raw materials to transform them in a way that will materialize the productive idea he had in mind.

So, too, practical thinking, or thinking in order to act purposefully or to do what is necessary to achieve some end or goal, falls short of actual doing. Doing begins when practical thinking is put into practice. Productive thinking may continue while production is actually going on. Practical thinking may continue during the course of purposeful action. But until making and doing actually begin, productive thinking and practical thinking bear no fruit.

Aristotle tells us that, except for the exceptional instances of aimless behavior, human beings always act with some end in view. The thinking they do in order to act purposefully begins with thinking about the goal to be achieved, but when they begin to do anything to achieve that goal, they have to start with the means for achieving it. The end comes first in the thinking that individuals do in order to act purposefully, but the means come first in what they do to accomplish their purposes.

In saying that human beings always—or usually—act with some end in view, Aristotle also says that they act for some good they wish to obtain and possess. He identifies an end being aimed at with a good that is desired.

In his view, it makes no sense at all to say that we are acting for an end that we regard as bad for us. That amounts to saying that what we are aiming at is something we do not desire. It is plain common sense that what we regard as bad for us is something we desire to avoid, not something we desire to possess.

What about the means we need to achieve the end we have in mind? To aim at an end is to seek a good that we desire. Are the means we must use to achieve the end also goods that we desire? Yes and no. The means are good, but not because we desire them for their own sake, but only because we desire them for the sake of something else.

Must we always regard means as good because they provide us with a way of getting the end we want to achieve? Certainly, means are good only if they do help us succeed in reaching our goal. But if they have other consequences, too, then they may be undesirable for reasons quite apart from achieving the end we have in mind.

Stealing would get the money that I need to buy an automobile I want, but stealing might also get me into serious trouble that I would wish to avoid. The means we use to attain the end we seek must not only be good because they get us where we want to go, but they must also not land us where we do not want to be—in jail.

To sum up: means may be an end that we have to achieve by other means, and an end may also be a means to some further end. These two observations lead to two questions that Aristotle thinks we cannot avoid. One is: Are there any means that are purely or merely means, never ends? The other is: Are there any ends that are ends and never means—what Aristotle calls ultimate or final ends because they are not means to any ends beyond themselves?

Another way of asking the first question is to ask whether there are any things that we desire only for the sake of something else, never for their own sake. And another way of asking the second question is to ask whether there are any things that we desire only for their own sake and never for the sake of something else.

Aristotle maintained that there are means that are merely or purely means, ends that are also means to goals beyond themselves, and ends that we pursue for their own sake and not for the sake of any further good to be obtained. His reasons for thinking so are as follows.

If there were nothing that we desired for its own sake and not for the sake of something else, our practical thinking could not begin. We have already seen that practical thinking must begin with thinking about an end to be sought or pursued. Now if every end we thought about were a means to some further end, and if that further end were still a means to some end beyond itself, and so on *endlessly,* practical thinking could never begin.

We have seen that when practical thinking is put into practice, we must start with some means to whatever end we have in view. If that means is itself an end that requires us to find means for achieving it, then we cannot start our doing, or purposeful action, with it. To start doing, we must start with a means that is purely a means, and not also an end that requires other means to achieve it.

So far I have told you only *why* there must be ends that are not means and why there must be means that are not ends. Your reaction to what I have told you so far would not surprise me if it consisted in wondering how you have ever done any practical thinking without knowing what your final or ultimate end is. If practical thinking cannot begin with an end that is a means to something beyond itself, and if you do not know of any end that you seek for its own sake and not for the sake of anything else, how could you ever begin to think practically? Since you have undoubtedly done a lot of practical thinking in the course of your life, Aristotle must be wrong when he says that practical thinking cannot begin until you have an ultimate or final end in mind.

So it would certainly seem. A distinction between two ways in which you can have an ultimate or a final end in mind will open the door to a solution of this problem. To get some understanding of the required distinction, let's start with what we learned in school about geometry—the same kind of geometry with which Aristotle was acquainted.

What we called the first principles of geometry are the starting points with which you must begin in order to demonstrate the geometrical propositions that have to be proved. In Euclid's geometry, the first principles consist of definitions, axioms, and postulates. The definitions of points, lines, straight lines, triangles, and so on are needed, and so are such axioms as "the whole is greater than any of its parts" and "things equal to the same thing are equal to each other." In addition, there are the postulates—assumptions that Euclid makes in order to prove the propositions that need proof.

The difference between the axioms and the postulates is that you cannot deny the axioms. You cannot avoid affirming them. For example, try to think that a part is greater than the whole to which it belongs. But when Euclid asks you to assume that you can draw a straight line from any point to any point, you may be willing to make that assumption, but you do not have to do so. There is nothing compelling about it as there is about the axiom concerning wholes and parts.

As axioms and postulates are different kinds of starting points in geometrical thinking, so are there different kinds of starting points in practical thinking. Just as you can assume what Euclid asks you to take for granted in order to get his geometrical proofs started, so in your own practical thinking, you can assume that a certain goal or end is ultimate, and ask no further questions about it, *even if they can be asked.*

In other words, most of us get started in our practical thinking not by having in mind that which is absolutely our final or ultimate goal, but rather by assuming that the end we have in view can be taken—for the time being at least—*as if* it were a goal about which no further questions need be asked.

In the example we have been considering, we may take being able to drive to school or to work as the end for which having an automobile, being able to buy it, getting the money needed to buy it, and so on, are the means. Of course, you realize that you could be asked why you want to drive to school or to work, and your answer to that question might lead to a further *why* until you came to an answer about which no further *why* could be asked.

That answer, if you ever reached it, would be your grasp of the ultimate or final end, for the sake of which everything else is a means. But you do not have to have such an end in view in order to begin practical thinking or purposeful doing because you can provisionally assume that some end you have in mind is, for the time being, ultimate—something you want for its own sake.

When you do what needs to be done to get it, you may ask yourself why you wanted it, but you do not have to ask that question in order to think about the means for getting it or in order to do what needs to be done to use means for that purpose. That question can be postponed—for the time being, but not forever, not, at least, if you want to lead a well-planned, purposeful life.

10

Living and Living Well

The younger we are, the more things we do aimlessly. If not aimlessly, then at least playfully. There is a difference between acting aimlessly and acting playfully. We act aimlessly when we have no end in view, no purpose. But when we behave playfully, we do have an aim—pleasure, the fun we get out of the game or whatever it is we are playing. The pleasure we get from the activity itself is our goal. We have no ulterior purpose; that is purpose enough.

Serious activity, as contrasted with playful activity, always has some ulterior purpose. We engage in the activity to achieve some goal, for which doing this or that is a means. Having and not having an ulterior purpose is one distinction between work and play, about which I will have more to say later. We all recognize that work is a serious activity and that it is seldom as pleasant as play.

The younger we are, the less likely it is that we will have a well-worked-out plan for living. When we are young, our goals are likely to be immediate ones—things to do, things to get, things to be enjoyed today, tomorrow, or next week at the most. Having such goals is hardly a plan for living one's life as a whole. One's life as a whole is a very difficult thing to think about when one is young.

As we get older, we become more and more purposeful. We also become more serious and less playful. That is generally true, but not true of everyone. There are exceptions. Some older persons live only for pleasure and enjoyment, and when we say that about them, we are not complimenting them. On the contrary, we are criticizing them for devoting too much of their time and energies to playing and not enough to serious activities. We are saying that the grown-up person who lives this way is not really grown-up but childish. It is all right for children to play a large part of the time, but not for mature men and women.

As we grow older and more purposeful, less playful and more serious, we try to fit all our various purposes together into a coherent scheme for living. If we don't, we should, Aristotle tells us. We should try to develop a plan for living in order to live as well as possible.

Socrates, who was Plato's teacher as Plato was Aristotle's, said that an unexamined life is not worth living. Aristotle went further and said that an unplanned life is not worth examining, for an unplanned life is one in which we do not know what we are trying to do or why, and one in which we do not know where we are trying to get or how to get there. It is a jumble, a mess. It is certainly not worth examining closely.

In addition to not being worth examining, an unplanned life is not worth living because it cannot be lived well. To plan one's life is to be thoughtful about it, and that means thinking about ends to be pursued and the means for achieving them. Living thoughtlessly is like acting aimlessly. It gets you nowhere.

But Aristotle does not think it is enough to persuade you that you must have a plan for living in order to live well. He also wishes to persuade you that you must have the right plan. One plan is not as good as another. There are lots of wrong plans, but only one right plan. If you adopt one of the wrong plans, you will end up, Aristotle thinks, not having had a good life. To end up having had a good life, you must have lived it according to the right plan.

The right plan? It may be easy for Aristotle to persuade us that we ought to have a plan for living in order to live thoughtfully and purposefully. That's just common sense. But for Aristotle to persuade us that there is only one right plan that we ought to adopt is not so easy. If he can succeed in doing that, it will be another indication of his uncommon common sense.

What can possibly make one plan for living right and all others wrong? To that question, Aristotle thinks there can be only one answer. The right plan is the one that aims at the right ultimate end—the end that all of us ought to aim at. That may be the answer to the question, but it leaves a further question unanswered. What is the right ultimate end—the end that all of us ought to aim at? You can see at once that if there were a right ultimate end, we ought to aim at it. Just as we find it impossible to think that part of a whole is greater than the whole of which it is a part, so we find it impossible to think that a wrong end is one we ought to aim at. If a goal is wrong, we ought not try to achieve it. Only if it is right, ought we to try.

Granted, you may say, but that still leaves the important question unanswered. What is the right ultimate end? What is the one goal that all of us ought to seek?

You may think that that is a hard question to answer, but Aristotle doesn't. Perhaps I should say that one of his answers to that question is very easy for him to give. But it is not the complete answer. The complete answer is much harder to state and to grasp. Let's start with the easier, though incomplete, answer.

The right end that all of us ought to pursue is a good life. Aristotle's reasoning on this point is simple and, I think, convincing. Let me summarize it.

There are certain things we do in order just to live—such things as nourishing and caring for our bodies and keeping them healthy, for the sake of which most of us have to work to earn the money we need to buy food, clothing, and shelter.

There are other things we do in order to live well. We make the effort to get an education because we think that knowing more than is necessary just to keep alive enriches our life. We do not need certain pleasures in order to keep alive, but having them certainly makes life richer and better.

Both living and living well are ends for which we have to find the means. But living, or keeping alive, is itself a means to living well. It is impossible to live well without staying alive—as long as possible or, at least, as long as it seems desirable to do so.

Living, I have just said, is a means to living well. But what is living well a means to? There can be no answer to that question, Aristotle tells us, because living well is an end in itself, an end we seek for its own sake and not for the sake of anything else or for any ulterior purpose.

Anything else that we can think of, anything else that we call good or desirable, is a means either to living or to living well. We can think of living as a means to living well, but we cannot think of living well as a means to anything else.

Aristotle thinks that that should be obvious to all of us. He also thinks that our common experience shows that all of us do, in fact, agree about it.

The word he uses for living well (or for a good life) has usually been translated into English by the word "happiness." Happiness, Aristotle says, is that which everyone seeks. No one, if asked whether he wants happiness, would say, "No, I want misery instead."

In addition, no one, if asked why he wants happiness, can give a reason for wanting it. The only reason for wanting it would have to be some more ultimate end, for the achievement of which happiness is a means. But no more ultimate end exists. There is nothing beyond happiness, or a good life, for which happiness can serve as a means.

I have used the word "happiness" as interchangeable with "living well" or "a good life." What has been said about happiness is not as plain and obvious if the word is used with any other meaning. I can avoid using the word "happiness" with any other meaning, but I cannot avoid using the word "happy" with many different meanings, meanings that are related to happiness in different ways.

We ask one another "Did you have a happy childhood?" We ask one another "Do you feel happy now?" We say to one another "Have a happy vacation" or "Have a happy New Year." When we use the word "happy" in these ways, we are talking about the pleasure or satisfaction that we experience when we get what we desire.

People who feel contented because they have what they want feel happy. A happy time is one filled with pleasures rather than pains, with satisfactions rather than dissatisfactions. That being so, we can be happy today and unhappy tomorrow. We can have a happy time on one occasion and an unhappy time on another.

Different human beings want different things for themselves. Their desires are not alike. What one person desires, another may wish to avoid. That amounts to saying that what some persons regard as good for themselves, others may regard as bad.

We differ in our desires and, therefore, we differ in what we regard as good for us. What makes one person feel happy may do just the opposite for another.

Since different persons feel happy as the result of doing different things or as the result of getting the different things they desire, how can it be said that happiness—living well or a good life—is the one right goal or ultimate end that all human beings ought to pursue?

Aristotle may be able to persuade us that all of us want happiness. He may be able to persuade us that we all want happiness for its own sake and not for the sake of anything else. But how can he persuade us that all of us, wanting happiness for its own sake, want exactly the same thing?

Human beings, in seeking happiness, certainly appear to be seeking different things. That is a matter of common experience, which Aristotle acknowledged without hesitation. He knew from common experience, as we do, that some individuals think that achieving happiness consists in accumulating great wealth; others, that it consists in having great power or becoming famous and having lots of fun.

If happiness, like feeling happy, results from getting what you want, and if different persons want different things for themselves, then the happiness to be achieved must be different for different persons.

If that is so, then how can there be one right plan for living well? How can there be one ultimate end that everyone ought to pursue? Happiness or living well may be the ultimate end that all of us seek, but it is not the same end for all of us.

Please remember something I said earlier in this chapter. I said that there was an easy, but incomplete, answer to the question, What is the one right ultimate end that all of us should seek? The easy but incomplete answer is: happiness, living well, or a good life as a whole. To get at the complete answer, we must see if Aristotle can show us why living well, a good life, or happiness is the same for all of us.

II

Good, Better, Best

We know from common experience that individuals differ in their desires. We also know that in our everyday speech we use the word "good" as a label for the things we regard as desirable.

If we look upon one thing as more desirable than another, we regard it as better. And of several desirable things, the one we desire most is best in our eyes.

Reflection on these facts of common experience and common speech led Aristotle to the common-sense conclusion that the two notions—the good and the desirable—are inseparably connected. As axiomatic as Euclid's "the part is less than the whole" and "the whole is greater than the part" are "the good is desirable" and "the desirable is good."

Let me remind you now of the problem we left unsolved at the end of the preceding chapter. We saw that differences in human desires make it difficult for Aristotle to persuade us that all human beings have the same end in view when they aim at living well, at a good life, or happiness. What one human being thinks will achieve happiness might be quite different from what another thinks a good life consists of. That being so, how can Aristotle uphold his view that there is only one right plan for living well or for attaining happiness?

He cannot do so unless he can help us understand that human desires are not all of the same sort, and that what is true of one kind of desire is not true of another kind.

The kind of desires that we have been considering so far are individual desires, desires acquired in the course of an individual's life and experience. Since individuals differ from one another not only in their temperaments and dispositions but also in the lives they lead and their special experiences, they differ in their acquired, individual desires.

While each human being is a unique individual with a unique life and unique experience, all human beings, as members of the human species, share in a common humanity. The multitude and variety of individual differences overlie the common traits or attributes that are present in all human beings because they are all human.

For the most part, these differences are differences in degree. All human beings have eyes and ears, are able to see and hear, but one individual's vision or hearing may be more acute than another's. All human beings have the ability to reason, but that common ability may be greater in one individual than in another. All human beings need food for sustenance and vitality, but one individual, being of larger build than another, may need more nourishment than another.

The last example of a common trait underlying individual differences calls attention to the other kind of desire—a kind of desire that is natural, not acquired, and that is the same in all human beings, not different in different individuals, except in degree. When we say that we *need* food, we are saying that we desire food, just as much as when we say that we *want* a new automobile, we are saying that we desire it. These two words—"need" and "want"—both indicate desires, but not desires of the same kind.

Needs are inborn or innate desires—desires inherent in our human nature because we have certain natural capacities or tendencies, capacities or tendencies common to us all because we all have the same human nature. We all have a biological capacity for nourishment. All plants and animals have that capacity; stones do not. That is why all living things need food. Without it, they die. The fulfillment of the capacity is necessary to sustain life.

The individual does not acquire the desire for food in the course of his lifetime or as a result of his own special experience. He needs food whether he knows it or not, and he needs it even when he does not feel the need, as he does when he has pangs of hunger. Hunger is merely the experience of feeling a natural need that is always present and present in all.

Individuals born in Asia, Africa, Europe, and North America all have the same need for food and drink, and all will, on certain occasions, experience pangs of hunger and thirst. But born in different environments and growing up under different circumstances, these different individuals will acquire desires for different kinds of food and drink. When they feel hungry or thirsty (which is their awareness of a natural need), they will want different kinds of edibles and drinkables to satisfy their desire.

They do not *need* different kinds of edibles and drinkables. They *want* them. If the kind of food or drink they want were not available, their need could be satisfied by food and drink they do not want because they have not yet acquired a desire for it.

The example we have been considering is a biological need, a need common not only to all human beings but also to all living things. Let us now consider a peculiarly human need, one that is common only to human beings because it arises from a capacity that is a special attribute of human nature.

Earlier in this book, I suggested that human beings differ from other animals by their capacity for asking questions with the aim of acquiring knowledge about themselves and about the world in which they live. Recognizing this fact, Aristotle begins one of his most important books with the sentence: "Man by nature desires to know." He is saying, in other words, that the desire for knowledge is as much a natural need as the desire for food.

However, there is one interesting difference between the need for knowledge and the need for food. Deprived of food, most human beings are conscious of that deprivation when they feel the pangs of hunger. But deprived of knowledge, it is not always the case that human beings are conscious of their deprivation. Unfortunately, we seldom experience the pangs of ignorance as we feel the pangs of hunger.

All acquired desires are desires we are conscious of when we have them. That is not true of all natural needs. Some of them, like the need for food and drink, we are conscious of when we are deprived of what we need. But other natural needs, like the need for knowledge, we may or may not be conscious of, even when we are deprived of what we need.

The fact that we are not conscious of a natural need should not lead us into the mistake of thinking that the need of which we are unaware does not exist. It is there whether or not we are aware of it.

I have given a few examples of natural needs in order to contrast them with acquired wants and in order to illustrate Aristotle's distinction between two kinds of desire. It is not necessary here to try to give you an exhaustive enumeration of the natural needs that all human beings share in common, as they share in common all the potentialities, capacities, and tendencies that are inherent in their specific human nature. My present interest is in showing how Aristotle's distinction between two kinds of desires will help him to persuade us that there is one right plan for living well that all of us ought to adopt.

To understand his argument, we must recognize what I think all or most of us do recognize—that we often want things we do not need. We even make the mistake of saying that we need them when we only want them. No one needs caviar, but many people, having acquired the taste for it, want it; and they may even allow themselves to say they need it.

That is not the only mistake you can make about your wants. You can also want something that is not really good for you. Some human beings want drugs or other substances that are harmful to them. They have acquired strong desires for these things and want them so strongly that they ignore the injury they are doing themselves. They want something that is bad for them. But because they want it, it appears good to them at the time they are seeking to gratify their desires.

If it did not appear good to them, it would be false to say that the desirable is good. When they desire that which is really bad for them, it nevertheless appears good to them. Their desire or want was wrong or mistaken. That is why that which appeared good to them was not really good.

In contrast to the things you want, which appear good at the time you want them but may turn out to be the opposite of good at a later time, the things you need are *always* good for you. Because they are really good for you, they are not good at one time and the opposite at another.

You may be mistaken in thinking that you need something when you only want it—caviar, for example—but your needs are never wrong or misdirected, as your wants may be and often are. You cannot have a wrong or mistaken need. And anything you need is something really good for you, not something that merely appears to be good at a certain time because you desire it.

We now see that Aristotle's distinction between natural and acquired desires (or between needs and wants) is closely related to another distinction he makes—between real and apparent goods. The things that are really good for you are the things that satisfy your natural needs. The things that only appear to be good for you, and may not be really good for you, are the things that satisfy your acquired wants.

Another way of making this point is to say that apparent goods are the things we call good because we do in fact consciously desire them at the time. We want them. Because we want them, they appear good to us and we call them good. In contrast, real goods are things we need, whether we are conscious of the need or not. Their goodness consists in their satisfying a desire inherent in human nature.

There is still one other way of making the same point, and it is worth considering because it advances our understanding of Aristotle's argument. The good is the desirable and the desirable is good. But a thing may be desirable in two different senses of "desirable," just as it may be good in two senses of "good." We can call something desirable because at a given time we do in fact desire it. Or we can call something desirable because we ought to desire it whether, at a given time, we actually desire it or not.

What is desirable in one sense may not be desirable in the other. We may actually desire what we ought not to desire, or in fact fail to desire what we ought to desire. That which is really good for us is something we always ought to desire because we need it, and we cannot have wrong needs. But that which only appears to be good for us is something that may be wrong for us to desire. It may be something we ought not to desire because it will turn out to be really bad for us even though, at the time we want it, it appears to be good because we want it.

The one right plan for achieving happiness or a good life is, according to Aristotle, a plan that involves us in seeking and acquiring all the things that are really good for us to have. They are the things we need not only in order to live but also in order to live well. If we seek all the real goods that we ought to possess in the course of our lives, we will be pursuing happiness according to the one right plan of life that we ought to adopt.

Since natural needs, based on our common human capacities and tendencies, are the same in all human beings, what is really good for any one person is really good for any other. That is why human happiness is the same for all human beings: it consists in the possession of all the things that are really good for a person to have, accumulated not at one time but in the course of a lifetime. And that is why the one right plan for living well is the same for all human beings.

No human life can be completely deprived of real

goods, for on the biological level the total deprivation of basic needs would make it impossible to stay alive for long. The biological needs for food, drink, clothing, shelter, and sleep must be satisfied, at least to a minimal extent, in order for the living organism to stay alive. But when those needs are satisfied to that minimal extent and no more, just staying alive—or bare subsistence—serves poorly as a means to living well.

Not only must these basic biological needs be satisfied beyond the level of the barest minimum required to sustain life itself but, in addition, many other human needs must be satisfied in order to approach the fulfillment of all our human capacities and tendencies. If happiness consists in such complete fulfillment, then one individual approaches more closely to achieving it in proportion as he is more able than another to satisfy his human needs and come into the possession of the things that are really good for him.

One plan for living well is better than another to the extent that it guides the individual to a more complete realization of his capacities and to a more complete satisfaction of his needs. And the best plan of all, the one we ought to adopt, is one that aims at every real good in the right order and measure and, in addition, allows us to seek things we want but do not need, so long as getting them does not interfere with our being able to satisfy our needs or fulfill our capacities.

Not all apparent goods—things that we want but do not need—turn out to be bad for us. Some are not injurious in themselves; and some are not disadvantageous in the sense that they impede or frustrate our effort to get the things that we need and that are really good for us. The pursuit of happiness by one man may differ from its pursuit by another even if both are following the one right plan for living well.

The reason for such differences, when they occur, is that each individual may want different things for himself over and above the things he needs. Though what is really good for one human being is the same for all, what appears to be good to one individual, according to his wants, may be quite different from what appears to be good to another individual. What each individual wants for himself may be an apparent good that is neither injurious to him nor an impediment to his pursuit of happiness.

You now have some grasp of Aristotle's views about happiness and how it should be pursued. You see why he thinks it is the same for all human beings and why all should try to achieve it by adopting the one sound plan for doing so. Other questions remain to be answered.

What are the real goods that an individual should seek in order to live well or make a good life for himself or herself? We have mentioned some of them, but not all. Can the enumeration of real goods be completed?

If it can be, then there is still a further question—the most important of all: How should we try to come into possession of all the things we naturally need—all the real goods we should have in our lives? What means are indispensable to achieving the ultimate end we have in mind?

Only when these questions have been answered will we have a full grasp of the plan of life to be followed in order to achieve happiness.

12

How to Pursue Happiness

When Thomas Jefferson drafted the Declaration of Independence, did he understand Aristotle's view of happiness and how to pursue it?

The Declaration says that all human beings, being equal by nature, have an equal right to life, liberty, and the pursuit of happiness. Living, we have seen, is itself a means to living well. So is freedom.

Unless we can exercise a free choice about the things we want or need, and unless we can freely carry out the choices we make—without coercion or impediment—we cannot pursue happiness. If everything is determined for us, if the pattern of our life is imposed upon us, there would be no sense in talking about planning our lives or about adopting a plan for living well.

We need to stay alive in order to live well. We need liberty in order to make an effort—a planned effort—to live well. Because we need these things in order to pursue happiness, we have a right to them. But do we need to pursue happiness? Do we need to live well? If not, what is the basis for saying, as Jefferson did, that all human beings have a right—a right inherent in their human nature—to pursue happiness?

The answer to that question lies in a number of points that were covered in the preceding chapters. Living well, or happiness, we saw, is the ultimate or final end of all our doing in this life—that which we seek for its own sake and for the sake of no further good beyond it. We also saw that we do in fact desire certain things and when we do, they appear good to us. There are other things we ought to desire because they are really good for us, whether or not they appear to be so at the time.

Now if a good life as a whole is one that involves having all the things that are really good for us, then we ought to desire to live well—to achieve happiness or a good life. Since anything that is really good for us is something we ought to desire, the sum total of real goods is certainly something we ought to desire.

The word "ought" expresses the notion of a duty or an obligation. We have a duty or an obligation to do what we ought to do. To say that we ought to pursue happiness as the ultimate goal of our life is to say that we have a duty or obligation to try to live well or to make a good life for ourselves.

To fulfill that duty or obligation, we need whatever is indispensable to making a good life for ourselves—we need the real goods that, taken all together, constitute or make up happiness or a good life. That is why we have a right to them. If we did not have the obligation to try to live well and if we did not need certain things in order to do so, we would not have the right to them that Thomas Jefferson asserted all of us have.

Thomas Jefferson thought that all human beings, having the same human nature, had the same natural rights. That amounts to saying that they all have the same natural needs—that what is really good for any one human being is really good for all human beings. To this extent, Thomas Jefferson appears to have adopted Aristotle's view that the pursuit of happiness involves all human beings in seeking and trying to obtain the same set of real goods for themselves.

Before I attempt to enumerate the real goods that Aristotle thought all of us should seek, I would like to spend a moment on the difference between the question "What should I do in order to pursue happiness?" and the question "What steps should I take in order to make a chair, a picture, or a piece of music?" The difference between these two questions throws light on the difference between doing and making, and between the kind of thinking that is involved in acting in order to live well and the kind of thinking that is involved in producing something that is well made.

If you undertake to make a chair, a picture, or a piece of music, you must have a productive idea of the thing to be made and you must have the know-how or the skill required to produce a well-made chair, picture, or piece of music. The productive idea and the know-how are the means to that end. But you are under no obligation to seek that end. Only *if* you are determined to make that particular chair, picture, or piece of music must you employ the means required to produce it.

Pursuing happiness is different from producing a chair, picture, or piece of music because you do not begin by saying, "If I wish to pursue happiness, I must do this or that." There is no *if* about it, as there is in the case of the chair, the picture, or the piece of music. You may not wish to produce a particular chair, nor need you, but you ought to pursue happiness. That is why there is no *if* about it.

You ought to pursue happiness, but how ought you go about doing so? This is the question that remains to be answered.

Aristotle offers us two related answers to that question. The first answer consists in his enumeration of the real goods that all of us need—the goods that, taken together, constitute happiness or a good life as a whole. The second answer consists in his prescription for obtaining all the real goods we need in the course of a lifetime. The first answer is easier than the second, so let us start with it.

We are, by nature, questioning, thinking, and knowing animals. As animals, we have bodies that need to be cared for in certain ways. As human animals, we have minds that need to be exercised in certain ways. Some of the real goods we need Aristotle calls bodily goods, such as health, vitality, and vigor. And since our senses give us the experience of bodily pleasures and pains, Aristotle also includes such pleasures among the real goods. Few of us, I think, would challenge his common-sense observations that we ought to seek bodily pleasure and ought to avoid, if we can, bodily pain.

These bodily goods are goods we share with other animals. They are goods for us because we are animals. It is only in the way that we seek them that we differ from other animals. For example, other animals instinctively try to avoid bodily pain and always instinctively try to enjoy bodily pleasure. By watching a pet cat or dog, you will see that this is so. But human beings sometimes give up bodily pleasure or endure bodily pain for the sake of some other good that they think is more desirable. And we may even think it advisable for us to limit our enjoyment of bodily pleasure in order to make room in our lives for other, more important goods.

The bodily goods that have been mentioned are means to the ultimate end of happiness or a good life. But they are also themselves ends for which other goods serve as means. For the sake of our bodily health, vitality, and pleasure, we need food, drink, shelter, clothing, and sleep.

Aristotle lumps all these things together under one heading which he calls external goods or wealth. Wealth, according to Aristotle, is a real good because it is a necessary means to bodily health, vitality, and pleasure. Without a certain amount of wealth, we cannot enjoy health, vitality, or pleasure, and without these things we cannot live well.

Individuals who are starving, who are freezing or sweltering, individuals who are deprived of sleep or whose bodies are consumed by the effort to keep alive from moment to moment, individuals who lack the externals that give them the simple comforts of life, cannot live well. They are as badly off as individuals who are forced to work as slaves, who are in chains, or who are confined by prison walls. The lack of a certain amount of wealth is as much an obstacle to living well and achieving happiness as the deprivation of a certain amount of freedom.

In both cases I have said, as Aristotle would say, "a certain amount." He does not say that unlimited freedom is needed to live well, nor does he say that unlimited wealth is needed. The reason for the limitation is not the same, but both are limited, not unlimited, goods, just as bodily pleasure is also a limited good, of which we can want too much for our own ultimate good.

To the two kinds of goods that have already been mentioned—bodily goods and external goods, or wealth—Aristotle adds a third. These goods he calls goods of the soul. We might refer to them as psychological goods, as we would probably refer to the goods of the body as physical goods.

The most obvious of these psychological goods are goods of the mind, such as knowledge of all sorts, including know-how and skill. Among the skills all of us need is certainly the skill of thinking. We need it not only in order to produce well-made things, but also in order to act well and live well.

Less obvious, perhaps, are the psychological goods that we need because we are social animals as well as thinking animals. We cannot live well in complete solitude. A solitary life is not a good life, any more than the life of a slave or of a man in chains is a good life.

Just as we naturally desire to acquire knowledge, so we naturally desire to love other human beings and to be loved by them. A totally loveless life—a life without friends of any sort—is a life deprived of a much-needed good.

Even though other human beings are as external to ourselves as the various forms of wealth are, Aristotle does not place friendship among the external goods. He treats it rather as a psychological good—a good of the soul. Because it fulfills a psychological need on our part, friendship is like knowledge and skill rather than like the things that satisfy our bodily needs.

There are pleasures of the mind as well as pleasures of the body. Among them, for example, is the pleasure we get from making things and from our enjoyment of works of art—things that are well made by others. There is also the satisfaction we feel in acquiring knowledge, in having skills of one sort or another, and in loving and being loved.

Human beings desire to be loved. They also wish to be respected for the traits they think admirable or lovable. Recognizing this, Aristotle includes, among the goods that contribute to a good life, self-esteem and honor. But, in his view, being honored is not a real good unless it is for the right reason—unless we really deserve the honor we receive. Some individuals seek fame instead of honor. They are satisfied with having a good reputation even if they do not deserve it.

I have now almost completely enumerated the real goods that Aristotle thinks go to make a good life as a whole. They are the component parts of that whole, and as such they are the means we must use to achieve that whole for ourselves. This is Aristotle's first answer to the question about how to succeed in achieving happiness. To the extent that we manage to obtain and possess all these real goods, we succeed in our effort to live well and make a good life for ourselves.

Aristotle's second answer to the same question involves a different kind of prescription for us to follow. It directs us to act in such a way that we develop a good moral character. Over and above all the real goods that have so far been mentioned, there is one more class of goods that we need—good habits; more specifically, good habits of choice.

Persons who have developed the skill of playing tennis well possess a good habit, one that enables them regularly to play well. Persons who have acquired the skill of solving problems in geometry or algebra have a good habit. So, too, have those who regularly and without difficulty restrain themselves from eating or drinking more than is good for them, or from indulging too much in the pleasures of sleep or play.

These are all good habits, but the good habits mentioned last are different from the others. Skill in playing tennis is a good bodily habit, and skill in solving mathematical problems with ease is a good habit of the mind. Good habits of this kind enable us to perform certain actions with excellence, not only regularly but also without effort. Contrasted with these habits of action are habits that enable us to make certain choices regularly, with ease, and without having to go through the process of making up our minds and deciding how to choose each time that we do so.

The person who has acquired the firm and settled disposition to avoid eating or drinking too much has a habit of this sort. It is a *good* habit because the decision to restrain oneself when tempted to overindulge in food and drink is the *right* decision.

Food and drink are real goods, but only in moderate amounts. There can be too much of many real goods, pleasures of all sorts. We often want more of them than is good for us, more than we need. That is why Aristotle tells us that we need good habits of choice or decision—in order to seek real goods in the right amount and also in order to seek them in the right order and in the right relation to one another.

The name that Aristotle gives to all good habits is a Greek word that can best be translated by the English word "excellence." However, that Greek word more frequently comes down to us in English by way of its Latin translation, and so the more usual English word for good habits is the word "virtue."

Good habits of the kind exemplified by skills of one sort or another are virtues of the mind, or intellectual virtues. Good habits of the kind exemplified by a settled disposition to choose or decide correctly constitute a person's character, and so Aristotle calls them moral virtues.

Both kinds of virtue are real goods that we need for a good life. But moral virtue plays a very special role in our pursuit of happiness, so special that Aristotle tells us that a good life is one that has been lived by making morally virtuous choices or decisions.

Why Aristotle thinks that statement sums it up I will try to explain in the next chapter.

Man the Doer 95

for you. Knowledge, skill, and the pleasures of the

13

Good Habits and
Good Luck

Some of the real goods that are required for a
good life are means to others. External goods, such as
food, clothing, and shelter, are means to health, vitality, and vigor. We need wealth to live well because we
need health to live well.

Similarly, we need health, vitality, and vigor in order to engage in activities that are necessary to obtain
still other goods. If we did not have to do anything at
all in order to live well, we would not need vitality and
vigor in order to be active.

In the order of goods, the highest ranking belongs
to those that we desire for their own sake as well as for
the sake of a good life. Wealth, for example, is not desirable for its own sake, but only as a means to living
well. But such real goods as friendship and knowledge
are desirable for their own sake as well as for the sake
of a good life.

Some real goods are limited goods; others are unlimited goods. For example, wealth and bodily pleasure
are limited goods. You can want more of them than
you need, and more than you need is not really good

for you. Knowledge, skill, and the pleasures of the mind are unlimited goods. More of them is always better. They are goods of which you cannot have too much.

If there were no limited goods of which you could want more than you need; *if* all real goods were equally important, so that none of them should be sought for the sake of any other; *if* wanting certain things that appear good to you did not come into conflict with seeking other things that are really good for you—*if* life could be lived this way, then there would be little or no difficulty about living a good life, and there would be no need for good habits of choice and decision in order to succeed in one's pursuit of happiness.

But that, Aristotle knew, is not the way it is. If you think about your own life for a moment, you will see that he was right. Just think about the regrets you have had. Remember the times you were sorry because you were too lazy to take the trouble to do what was necessary to get something you needed. Or remember when you allowed yourself the pleasure of oversleeping or overeating and regretted it later. Or the time when you did not do something you ought to have done because you feared the pain you might suffer in doing it.

If you had made the right choice and decision every one of those times, you would have no regrets. Choices and decisions that leave you with no regrets are choices and decisions that contribute to your pursuit of happiness by putting real goods in the right order, by limiting the amount when it should be limited, and by putting aside things you want if they get in the way of obtaining things you need.

Moral virtue, Aristotle tells us, is the habit of making right choices. Making one or two right choices among many wrong choices will not do. If the wrong choices greatly outnumber the right choices, you will be moving steadily in the wrong direction—away from achieving happiness instead of toward it. That is why Aristotle stresses the notion of habit.

You know how habits get formed. To form the

habit of being on time for appointments, you have to try to be punctual over and over again. Gradually, the habit of being punctual gets formed. Once it is formed, you have a firm and settled disposition to be on time in getting where you promised to be. The stronger the habit, the easier it is to act that way and the harder it is to break the habit or to act in an opposite fashion.

When you have formed a habit and it is well developed, you take pleasure in doing what you are in the habit of doing because you do it with ease—almost without effort. You find acting against your habits painful.

What I have just said is true of both good and bad habits. If you have formed the habit of oversleeping, it is easy and pleasant to turn the alarm clock off and go on sleeping. It is hard and painful to get up on time. So, too, if you have formed the habit of allowing yourself to overindulge in certain pleasures or to avoid taking certain pains, it is hard to stop doing it.

Such habits are bad habits, in Aristotle's view, because they interfere with your doing what you ought to do in order to get things you need. The opposite habits are good habits because they enable you to obtain what is really good for you instead of what only appears to be good for you at the time and may turn out to be bad for you in the long run.

Good habits, or moral virtues, are habits of making the right choices among goods, real and apparent. Bad habits, which Aristotle calls "vices," are habits of making the wrong choices. Every time you make a right choice and act on it, you are doing something that moves you toward your ultimate goal of living a good life. Every time you make a wrong choice and act on it, you are moving in the opposite direction. The virtuous person is one who makes the right choices regularly, time and time again, although not necessarily every single time.

That is why Aristotle thinks that virtue plays such a special role in the pursuit of happiness. That is why he regards moral virtue as the principal means to happiness and as the most important of all the things that are really good for us to have. Moral virtue is also an unlimited good. You cannot have too much of it. Habits of making right choices and decisions can never be too firmly formed.

Aristotle calls one aspect of moral virtue temperance. It consists in habitually resisting the temptation to overindulge in pleasures of all sorts or the temptation to seek more than is good for us of any limited good, such as wealth. One reason why bodily pleasures tempt us is that we can usually enjoy them right away. Having temperance enables us to resist what appears to be good in the short run for the sake of what is really good for us in the long run. Having temperance also enables us to seek wealth in the right amount—only as a means to other goods, and not for its own sake as if it were an end in itself and an unlimited good.

Aristotle calls another aspect of moral virtue courage. Just as temperance is an habitual disposition to resist the lure of pleasures for the sake of more important goods that overindulgence in pleasure would prevent us from getting, so courage is an habitual disposition to take whatever pains may be involved in doing what we ought to do for the sake of a good life.

For example, we recognize that getting knowledge and developing certain skills are intellectual virtues that we ought to have. But acquiring knowledge and skills may be painful. Studying is often hard to do; learning how to play a musical instrument well, how to write well, or how to think well involves practicing that is often irksome.

The habit of avoiding what is difficult or irksome because it is painful can certainly interfere with your acquiring knowledge and skills that are really good for you to have. That bad habit Aristotle calls the vice of cowardice.

The person who habitually avoids taking pains and trouble for the sake of obtaining real goods is as much a coward as the soldier who runs away in battle for fear of getting hurt. The soldier who risks his life or overcomes his fear of injury for the sake of victory in a good cause has courage. So, too, has anyone who habitually takes trouble, undergoes hardships, and suffers pain, in order to obtain things that are really good for him.

Temperance and courage differ as aspects of moral virtue. One is concerned with resisting the lure of bodily pleasures and with limiting our craving for limited goods. The other is concerned with suffering pains and hardships. But both are alike in one very important respect. Both are habits of making the right choice between things that only appear to be good and things that are really good. Both are habits of making the right choice between something that may be really good, but only in the short run of today, tomorrow, or next week, and something that is really good for us in the long run or for our life as a whole.

Aristotle realized that it is hard for those who are young in years of experience to keep their eyes on remote, future goods in relation to immediately present pleasures and pains. He knew that that is difficult even for those who are older. But he also reminded us that the difficulty of looking ahead to one's life as a whole is a difficulty all of us must overcome in trying to acquire moral virtue—the habit of choosing rightly between goods of lasting importance and transient pleasures and pains.

His pointing this out calls our attention to the fact that trying to live well is not easy for any of us. That does not make the goal any less desirable to attain. Nor does it relieve us of the obligation to make the effort. On the contrary, in Aristotle's view the satisfaction that comes from having succeeded in living a good life or in trying to live one is worth all the trouble and effort it takes.

However, a willingness to take the trouble and make the effort is not by itself enough. If an individual has the appropriate raw materials at his or her disposal and if he or she has the skill or know-how necessary for producing something that is well made, producing it is almost entirely within the individual's power. If individuals fail, the fault is theirs. Unfortunately, what is true of making a work of art is not true of living a good life.

Success in that venture is not entirely within our power. We can fail without being at fault. We can fail even if we have the moral virtue that Aristotle thought was requisite for success. Good habits of choice are requisite for success, but having them does not guarantee it.

The reason why this is so is that all the real goods we should seek to possess in order to live well are not entirely within our power to obtain. Some, such as good habits of mind and character (the intellectual and the moral virtues) are much more within our power to possess than others, such as wealth and health, or even freedom and friendship. Even acquiring knowledge and skill or forming good habits of choice may depend on having helpful parents and teachers, which is beyond our own control.

We are not able to control the conditions under which we are born and brought up. We cannot make fortune smile upon us. Much that happens to us happens by chance rather than by choice on our part.

Effort on our part does not assure us that we will come into possession of the external goods we need to live a good life. Nor does the care we take of our bodies assure us that we will retain our health and vigor. Poverty and disabling disease and even the loss of freedom and of friends can be our lot in spite of the most virtuous conduct on our part.

Moral virtue, however important it is for living a good life, is not enough because chance as well as choice plays a role in the pursuit of happiness. Good luck is as necessary as good habits. Some of the real goods we come to possess are largely the gift of fortune, though making a good use of them after we have them depends on our having good habits. That, in Aristotle's view, still makes mortal virtue the controlling factor in living a good life.

In addition, having good habits enables a person to bear up under misfortunes. If we cannot control what happens to us by chance, we can at least take advantage of the good things that fall into our lap as a result of good fortune; and we can try to make up for the things of which we are deprived by misfortune. Moral virtue helps us in both ways to deal with the twists and turns of fortune—good and bad.

Aristotle sums all this up when he says that our success in living a good life depends on two things. One is having the moral virtue that enables us to make right choices from day to day. The other is being blessed by good luck or good fortune. As moral virtue prevents us from aiming in the wrong direction and choosing things that are not really good for us, so good fortune supplies us with real goods that are not entirely within our power to obtain by choice.

A good life, it has been said, is one in which a person has everything that he or she desires, provided that he or she desires nothing amiss. In order to desire nothing amiss, one must have moral virtue. But one must also have goods that lie beyond the reach of choice—the goods bestowed on us by good luck, in addition to the goods acquired by good habits of choice.

Among these goods of fortune are things that depend on the physical environment and on the society in which we are born, brought up, and live our lives. Aristotle never lets us forget that we are social animals as well as physical organisms. Having a good family and living in a good society are as important as living in a good climate and having good air, good water, and other physical resources available.

Up to this point, we have been considering the pursuit of happiness as if it were a solitary affair—as if it were something each of us could do by himself or herself alone, with no thought of others. That is hardly the way things are. Since we cannot live well in complete solitude, we must think of what we have to do in order to live well with others. We must also think of what others can and should do to help us in our effort to lead a good life.

The pursuit of happiness is selfish to the extent that the good life it aims at directly is one's own good life, not the good life of anybody else. But when we realize that we cannot succeed in the pursuit of happiness without considering the happiness of others, our self-interest becomes enlightened. We cannot be entirely selfish and succeed.

That is why, according to Aristotle, the two aspects of moral virtue that we have so far considered are not enough. In addition to temperance and courage, there is justice. Justice is concerned with the good of others, not only of our friends or those whom we love, but of everyone else. Justice is also concerned with the good of the all-enveloping society in which we live—the society we call the state.

Living in a good society contributes greatly to the individual's pursuit of his own happiness because a good society is one that deals justly with the individuals who are its members. It also requires the individual to deal justly with other individuals and to act for the good of society as a whole. That good is a good in which all the members of society participate.

Persons who are not temperate and courageous injure themselves by habitually making the wrong choices. Persons who habitually make the wrong choices will also be unjust and injure others as well as the society in which they live. The reason for this is that those who firmly aim at a really good life for themselves will regularly make choices that carry out that aim. Choices so directed will also aim directly at a really good life for others and at the welfare of the society in which others share as well as themselves.

Consider, for example, the person who wants more wealth than is really good for him; or the person who overindulges his appetite for bodily pleasures; or the person who craves something that is not really good for anyone—power over other human beings in order to dominate their lives. Such persons will certainly ruin their own lives. It is also highly probable that they will injure others as a result of aiming in the wrong direction. But persons who aim their own lives in the right direction cannot help benefitting others and the society in which they live.

14

What Others Have a
Right to Expect
from Us

Aristotle said two things that seem to me uncommonly wise about the relation of one human being to another. Once understood, they are also common sense.

He said that if all men were friends, justice would not be necessary. He also said that justice is the bond of men in states.

Putting the two remarks together, we are led to conclude that the members of a state (which is the largest organized society to which we belong) are not all friends with one another. If they were, they would not need to be bound together by justice to form the society that we call a state.

Most of us belong to more than one society or organized group. We are members of a family, either as parents or children or as both. We may also belong to other organized groups, such as a school, a club, a business organization of one sort or another. All these are societies or associations of human beings who have combined with one another for some common purpose.

The purpose of the association distinguishes two of these organized groups from all the rest. Associations such as schools, universities, hospitals, business organizations, and clubs all aim at serving some particular good. Educational institutions, for example, aim at the dissemination and advancement of knowledge; hospitals, at the care of health; business organizations, at the production or distribution of things to be bought and sold; and so on.

In contrast, the family is a society that aims at sustaining the life of its members, and the state is a society that aims at enriching and improving that life. If there were no additional advantages to be derived from living in states, Aristotle thinks that human beings would have been content to continue living in the smaller society of the family or in the slightly larger society formed by a group of families, something like what we call a tribe. What led men to group families into tribes and group tribes into still larger societies was, in Aristotle's view, the advantages to be gained from the larger and more inclusive associations.

As we have seen, our aim as human beings should be not merely to stay alive but to live well—as well as possible. Staying alive, of course, is indispensable to living well. Not being solitary but social animals, human beings must associate with one another in order to sustain and preserve their lives and to bring into the world another generation that must be cared for and protected during infancy.

The family and the tribe, according to Aristotle, are the associations or societies that originally came into being to serve these purposes. They may not do so any longer, or not to the same extent, but Aristotle asks us to think about their origin. What caused human beings to form these associations in the first place?

One answer that may suggest itself is "instinct." Instinct causes bees to form beehives and ants to form ant colonies or ant mounds. Perhaps, then, it is a human instinct to form families, tribes, and states. If so, these societies would be completely natural, in contrast to such associations as schools, clubs, or business organizations. The latter are hardly the products of instinct. Men join together voluntarily to form these associations for the particular purposes they serve.

In Aristotle's view, families, tribes, and states are no more the products of instinct than are schools, clubs, and business organizations. They are not like beehives and ant mounds, which for a given species of bee or ant are always organized in exactly the same way, generation after generation, and wherever you find that particular species of bee or ant. But though all human beings belong to the same species, we find quite different patterns of association and organization in human families, tribes, and states.

That, according to Aristotle, indicates that these societies were, in origin, voluntarily and purposefully formed, and formed with some plan of organization that the human beings involved thought up for themselves. To this extent, they are like schools, clubs, and business organizations that human beings voluntarily, purposefully, and thoughtfully institute. But families, tribes, and states are also unlike schools, clubs, and business organizations because they are natural as well as voluntary.

Does not Aristotle contradict himself by saying that families, tribes, and states are both voluntary and natural? He would be contradicting himself if he thought that families, tribes, and states were natural in the same way that beehives and ant mounds are natural—the product of instinct. But, according to Aristotle, there is another way in which a society can be natural. It can be natural in the sense that it must be formed to serve some natural need—the need to stay alive or the need to live well.

A society can be natural in this sense and also be voluntarily, purposefully, and thoughtfully formed—to serve the need that makes the society natural.

Families, according the Aristotle, originated from the need of human beings to stay alive and to protect and rear their young. Groups of families, or tribes, being a little larger and involving more human beings working together, came into being in order to serve that same need a little more effectively. The even-larger organization of the state, which originally grew out of combinations of families and tribes, not only served that same need still more effectively but also served the additional purpose of enabling some individuals, if not all, to live well. Life itself being secure, attention and effort could be turned to improving life and making it richer and better.

When Aristotle says that man is by nature a political animal, he is saying more than is meant by the statement that man is a social animal. There are other social animals, such as bees and ants, wolves that hunt in packs, and lions that live in families. But only men organize their societies voluntarily, purposefully, and thoughtfully and establish laws or customs that differ from one human society to another.

That is one meaning of the statement that man is a political animal. He is a custom-making and law-making animal. There is another meaning. When Aristotle declares that man is by nature a political animal, he is also saying that human beings cannot live well, cannot achieve the best kind of lives for themselves, by living together only in families and in tribes. To do that, Aristotle thinks they must live together in cities or states.

The Greek word for a city or state is "polis," from which we get the English word "political." The Latin word for a city or state is "civis," from which we get the English words "civil" and "civilized." Being political by nature, men must live in states to live as well as possible. The good life is the civil or civilized life.

Now let us return to the two statements with which this chapter began. If all men were friends, justice would not be necessary. Since the members of a state are seldom if ever all friends with one another, justice is necessary to bind them together peacefully and harmoniously in that largest of all human societies—the state.

Let us, for the moment, suppose that the members

of a family are all friends with one another—friends in
the highest sense of that word.

When two human beings are friends in this
highest sense, they love each other. Their love impels
each of them to wish for the good of the other—to
wish to benefit the other, to do whatever may be necessary to improve or enrich the life of the other.

Each, out of such friendship or love, will act to
promote the happiness or good life of the other. Neither would do anything to injure the other by impeding
or obstructing the other's pursuit of happiness.

That is why justice would be unnecessary in a
family in which the parents loved their children, in
which the children loved their parents, and in which
husband and wife, brothers and sisters, loved one another perfectly and at all times. But in most families
there are times when love or friendship fails or falls
short of perfection. Then one member of the family
may say to another, "You are not being fair to me," or
"What you ask is unjust," or "I have a right to expect
this or that from you."

At such moments, love ceases to be the thing that
binds the members of the family together, and justice
enters the picture—justice that tries to see that the individual obtains what he or she has a right to expect,
that the individual is being fairly treated by the others,
and that he or she is protected from being harmed or
injured by them.

If justice did not intervene when love failed or fell
short of perfection, the members of the family might
not stay together, or at least they would not live together peacefully and harmoniously, trying to share in
the enjoyment of goods common to them all. What has
just been said is even truer of states in which the members are, for the most part, not related by friendship or
love. Where love is absent, justice must step in to bind
men together in states, so that they can live peacefully
and harmoniously with one another, acting and working together for a common purpose.

Aristotle knew that there are several different
kinds of friendship. Of these, he thought that only one
was perfect friendship—the kind that exists between

persons who love one another and wish only to benefit the other.

Aristotle also knew that such friendships are rare. More frequently, we speak of another person as being a friend because he is useful to us or because we get some pleasure from him. Such friendships are selfish. The person we call a friend serves some interest of our own, and we regard him or her as a friend only so long as that remains the case. In contrast, true friendship or love is unselfish. It is benevolent. It aims at serving the good of the other.

Justice, like love, is concerned with the good of the other person. However, there is a clear difference between them. Anyone who understands love knows that one individual should never say to another, "I have a right to be loved. You ought to love me."

When we truly love someone, we do not give the person loved what he or she has a right to claim from us. On the contrary, we give to them of ourselves generously and unselfishly, without any regard to their rights. We do for them more than they have any right to expect.

We sometimes even love persons who do not love us in return. We do not make their returning our love a condition for our loving them. But when we act justly toward others, giving them what they have a right to expect, we are selfish to the extent that we want justice from them in return. To say that we should do unto others what we would have them do unto us is selfish in this sense.

What do others have a right to expect from us? That we keep the promises we make to them. That we tell them the truth whenever telling a lie would hurt them in some way. That we return anything we have borrowed and promised to return. That we pay our debts to them. That we do not steal what belongs to them. That we do not injure their health, damage their bodies, or kill them. That we do not interfere with their freedom of action when their conduct in no way injures us. That we do not make false statements that would injure their reputation or give them a bad name.

All these things, and more of the same sort, can be summed up by saying that others have a right to expect from us that we do nothing that might impede or obstruct their pursuit of happiness—nothing that might interfere with or prevent their obtaining or possessing the real goods they need to make good lives for themselves. It is their need for these real goods that gives them a right to them, and it is their right to them that we are obliged to respect—if we ourselves are just.

We may not always be just, at least not perfectly just. Some persons are the very opposite of just. Instead of having the habit of respecting the rights of others, they are habitually inclined in the opposite direction—to get things they want for themselves even when to do so they must run roughshod over the rights of others.

That is why laws are made to prescribe what the members of a state should or should not do in order to deal justly with one another. If everyone had the habit of being just in all his dealings with others, there would be no need for such laws or for their enforcement by the state. But since few individuals are perfectly just, and since some are habitually inclined to be unjust, laws that prescribe just conduct must be enforced by the state to prevent one individual from seriously injuring another by violating his or her rights.

Do others have a right to expect us to act positively to help them in their pursuit of happiness? Not interfering with, impeding, or obstructing their efforts to obtain or possess the real goods they need is one thing. Helping them to obtain such goods is another. Have they a right to claim our help?

According to Aristotle's understanding of the difference between love and justice, the answer is no. It is the generosity of love, not the obligations of justice, that impels one individual to help another to obtain or possess the real goods needed for a good life. That is why the laws that the state enforces do not require individuals to help one another by taking positive action to promote the pursuit of happiness by others.

However, the state does make and enforce laws

that require the individual to act positively for the welfare of the community as a whole. The welfare of the community affects the pursuit of happiness by its members. A good society, a society in which the common good of the people is served and advanced, contributes to the good life of its individuals. Aristotle says in so many words that the end that the good state should serve is the happiness of the individuals who compose it. It should promote their pursuit of happiness.

When, therefore, we, as individuals, obey laws that direct us to behave for the welfare of the community as a whole, we are indirectly helping to promote the pursuit of happiness by our fellow human beings. What we do directly for a few others out of our love for them, we do indirectly for all the rest by obeying laws that require us to act for the welfare of the community in which they, as well as we, live.

15

What We Have a Right to Expect from Others and from the State

Love thy neighbor as thyself!

Do unto others as you would have them do unto you!

Both of these familiar maxims relate yourself to others. Both appear to make yourself the pivot of your action toward others. Love yourself and love your neighbor in the same way and even, perhaps, in the same measure as you love yourself. Think of how you wish others to behave toward you and behave in the same way toward them.

We seem to have reversed that order by considering first, in the preceding chapter, what others have a right to expect from us and now, in this chapter, what we have a right to expect from others. It would be more accurate to say that we have risen above an order that puts us first and others second.

Rights are rights. If any one human being has them, based upon needs that he or she shares in common with all other human beings, then all the others have the same rights, too. It makes no difference whether you think first of your own rights or first of the rights of others.

However, there is a sense in which you do come first. First in the order of thinking about what you should do. The ultimate goal that should control all your practical thinking, your choices, and your action is a good life for yourself. You are under an obligation to live as well as it is humanly possible to do—to obtain and possess, in the course of a lifetime, all the things that are really good for you.

Justice, as we have seen, does not require you to promote, by positive action on your part, the happiness of others, as you are required to pursue your own by the love you bear yourself. Justice only requires you not to impede or frustrate others in their pursuit of happiness. If you go beyond that to help them in their pursuit, you do so because you love them as you love yourself.

Your rights and the rights of others, with which justice is concerned, are based on the things that are really good for any human being because they fulfill needs inherent in human nature. Thinking about what is good, and especially about what is really good, must precede thinking about rights. For example, if you did not think that having a certain amount of wealth, having a satisfactory degree of health, and having freedom are really good for you, you would not be led to say that everyone has a right to these things, not only as means to living but also as means to living well.

What you have a right to expect from others is, therefore, the same as what they have a right to expect from you. Rights are the same because everyone's rights are the same and because what is really good for you is really good for every other human being. And that is so because all of us are human, all of us have the same human nature, inherent in which are the same fundamental needs calling for fulfillment.

Among those needs is the need to live in association with other human beings. We are not the kind of animal that can go it alone. As we have seen, human societies—families, tribes, and states—have arisen to fulfill this need. But they also help us to fulfill other needs—our need for goods on which the preservation of life itself depends and our need for higher goods on which living a good life depends.

Although society is itself good because we need to live in association with other human beings, a particular society may not be good if the way it is organized or the way it operates either fails to help or positively hinders individuals who are members of it in their efforts to acquire and possess things that are really good for them.

For example, a family is not a good family if it does not give the children in it the freedom they have a right to, if it does not care for their health, if it does not help them to grow up as they should. This does not mean that the family itself is a bad thing, for young children cannot preserve their own lives and grow up without families. It means only that a particular family is not good because it does not do for its children what they have a right to expect from it.

In his concern with what is good and bad, Aristotle is concerned with good and bad societies as well as with good and bad human beings and with their good and bad lives. What has already been said about society itself being good is, for him, a simple commonsense observation. We cannot get along at all without living in society.

Beginning there, Aristotle then goes on to consider what makes a particular society good or one society better than another. And just as his ultimate question about human life is about the best life that each of us can live, so his ultimate question about society is about the best society in which we can live and pursue happiness.

Since Aristotle thinks that, of all human societies, the state, or political society, is the one that most enables us to live the good or civilized life, let us concentrate on his answers to questions about the good state and the best state.

It seems obvious to him that a good state is one that is governed well. That, for Aristotle, is as obvious as it is to say that a good life is one that is lived well. For him, a state cannot exist without government. Human beings cannot live together peacefully and harmoniously in the absence of government.

That might not be true if all human beings were friends and loved one another. It might not even be true if all humans were perfectly just, so that there was no need for the enforcement of just laws to prevent one individual from injuring another. But Aristotle knew from common experience that all human beings are not bound together by love or friendship, that most human beings are not perfectly just, and that some are quite unjust in their selfishness.

That is why his common-sense conclusion was that government is necessary for the existence of a state or a political society.

Being necessary, government itself is good, just as society itself, being necessary, is good. However, as we have seen, a particular society may be bad or not as good as it should be. So, too, a particular form of government may be bad or not as good as it should be.

It has been said, by some who lack Aristotle's common sense, that government is not necessary at all. They fail to see that human beings—being as they are, not as one might wish they were—cannot live together peacefully and act together for a common purpose without living under a government having the power to enforce laws and to make decisions. It is not only that criminals must be restrained. In order that a number of individuals may act together for a common purpose, there must also be some machinery for making the decisions that their concerted actions require.

It has also been said that, although government may be necessary, it is a necessary evil because it involves the use of coercive force (the force used in the enforcement of laws) and because it involves limitations on the freedom of the individual. Those who say this fail to understand very important points that Aristotle makes about the enforcement of laws and about the limitations on the liberty of individuals in a society.

According to Aristotle, the good man—the virtuous man who is just—obeys just laws because he is virtuous, not because he fears the punishment that may follow from his breaking the law or disturbing the peace. He obeys laws and keeps the peace voluntarily, not under the coercion of law enforcement. He is not coerced by government, and so for him government is not an evil as it is for the bad man.

Nor does the good man feel that his freedom is limited by government. He does not want more freedom than he can use without injuring others. Only the bad man wants more freedom than that, and so only he feels that his freedom to do as he pleases, without regard for others, is limited by government.

The fact that government itself is necessary and good does not make all forms of government good, or as good as they should be. For Aristotle, the line that divides good from bad forms of government is determined by the answers to the following questions.

First, does the government serve the common good of the people who are governed, or does it serve the selfish interests of those who wield the power of government? Government that serves the self-interest of the rulers is tyrannical. Only government that promotes the good life of the ruled is good.

Second, does the government rest merely on the power at the disposal of the rulers, or does it rest on laws that have been made in a way to which the ruled have agreed and in the making of which they have had a part? Government that rests solely on might or force, whether it be in the hands of one man or more than one, is despotic, even when it is benevolent or well-disposed rather than tyrannical. To be good, government must have authority that those who are ruled acknowledge and accept, not merely power or force that they fear and submit to from fear.

Government that is good in this way Aristotle called constitutional government or political government. By calling such government political, he meant to suggest that it is the only form of government that is proper for states or political societies.

This brings us to a third question. It applies to government that is neither tyrannical nor despotic, but constitutional—a government based on laws, in which even those who govern are ruled by laws. About such government we have to ask: Is the constitution—the fundamental law on which government itself is based—a just constitution? And are the laws made by that government just laws?

Any government that is *not* tyrannical is *to that extent* good. Among nontyrannical governments, a constitutional government is better than a despotic one. And, among constitutional governments, the best is the one with a just constitution and with just laws.

In praising constitutional government, Aristotle speaks of it as the government of free men and equals. He also speaks of it as that form of government in which the citizens rule and are ruled in turn.

Those who are ruled by a despot are subjects, not citizens with some voice in their own government. Those who are ruled by a tyrant are no better off than slaves. In both cases, they are ruled as inferiors, not equals. Only those who, being citizens, are ruled by other citizens whom they have chosen to hold public office for a time are ruled as equals, and as free men should be ruled.

At this point in his thinking, Aristotle made a serious mistake. Living at a time and in a society in which some human beings were born into slavery and treated as slaves, as well as a society in which women were treated as inferiors, he made the mistake of thinking that many human beings had inferior natures. He did not realize that those who appeared to be inferior appeared to be so as the result of the way in which they were treated, not as a result of inadequate native endowments.

Making this mistake, he divided human beings into two groups. On the one hand, he placed those who were fit to be ruled as citizens—as free and equal and with a voice in their own government. On the other hand, he placed those who were fit only to be ruled despotically, either as subjects or slaves—without a voice in their own government and so as neither free nor equal.

We live at a time and in a society in which no one can be excused for making Aristotle's mistake. Correcting his mistake, we are led to the conclusion that all human beings should be governed as citizens with a voice in their own government and thus be ruled as free and equal. The only exceptions to that all-inclusive *all* are those who are still in their infancy or those who are mentally disabled.

Reaching this conclusion just stated, we also see that constitutional government is just only if its constitution gives all human beings the equal status of citizenship without regard to sex, race, creed, color, or wealth. In doing so, it also gives them the freedom they have a right to, the freedom of being ruled as citizens, not as slaves or subjects.

One human being is neither more nor less human than another, even though one may be superior or inferior to another in many other respects as a result of differences in native endowments or acquired traits. These inequalities should certainly be considered in the selection of some human beings rather than others to hold public office, but they should be totally disregarded in considering the qualifications for citizenship.

All human beings are equal as humans. Being equal as humans, they are equal in the rights that arise from needs inherent in their common human nature. A constitution is not just if it does not treat equals equally. Nor is it just if it does not recognize the equal right of all to freedom—to be ruled as human beings should be ruled, as citizens, not as slaves or subjects.

We now have reached one answer to the question about what we have a right to expect from the state in which we live and the government under which we live. We have a right to be ruled as citizens under a government to which we have given our consent and which allows us to have a voice in that government.

Is that all we have a right to expect? Even though

he made the mistake of thinking that only some human beings had the right to be ruled as citizens, Aristotle thought that those human beings had a right to expect more from the state in which they lived. The best state, in his opinion, was one that did everything it could do to promote the pursuit of happiness by its citizens. That remains true whether only some human beings or all should be citizens.

What can a state do to promote the pursuit of happiness by its citizens? It can help them to obtain and possess all the real goods that they need and have a right to. To understand this, we must remember one point made in the preceding chapter.

Of all the real goods we must have in order to live well, some are more and some are less within our individual power to acquire and possess. Some, like moral virtue and knowledge, depend largely on the choices we ourselves make. Some, like wealth and health, depend to a considerable extent on our having good luck or on our being blessed by good fortune.

The main ways in which a good state and a good government can help its individuals in their pursuit of happiness is to do what it can to overcome deprivations they suffer as a result of bad luck or misfortune, not as a result of fault on their part. It should do for them what they cannot, by choice and effort, do for themselves. The best state and the best government are those that do the most in this direction.

The one thing that no state or government can do, no matter how good it is, is to make its citizens morally virtuous. Whether or not they acquire moral virtue depends almost entirely upon the choices each of them makes. The best state and the best government can, therefore, only give its citizens external conditions that enable and encourage them to try to live well. It cannot guarantee that, given these conditions, they will all succeed. Their success or failure ultimately depends on the use they make of the good conditions under which they live their lives.

PART IV

MAN THE KNOWER

16

What Goes into the Mind and What Comes out of It

Earlier chapters have dealt with thinking and with knowing but not with the mind that thinks and knows.

In Part II, we considered productive thinking—the kind of thinking that is involved in the making of things. There we also considered the kind of knowledge needed for making—the kind we called skill or know-how.

In Part III, we examined practical thinking and practical knowledge—thinking about the means and ends of human action and knowledge of what is good and bad for us to seek, or right and wrong for us to do in the conduct of our lives.

Now, in Part IV, we will be concerned with theoretical thinking, thinking for the sake of knowing, not just for the sake of production or action. And we will be concerned with knowledge itself—with knowledge of the way things are as well as with knowledge of what we ought or ought not to do. Here for the first time we will consider what we know about the mind that thinks and knows.

Language plays a large part in human thinking and knowing. The words we use, according to Aristotle, express the ideas we think with. The declarative sentences we utter or the statements we make express opinions that we affirm or deny—opinions that may be either true or false.

When a statement we make happens to be true, it expresses knowledge. If it happens to be false, we have made an error. We cannot be in error about something and have knowledge about it at the same time. Opinions may be either true or false, correct or erroneous, but incorrect, erroneous, or false knowledge is as impossible as a round square.

Where do the ideas with which we think come from? It seemed obvious to Aristotle that we are not born with them in our minds—that they are somehow the products of our experience. That is why his account of human thinking and knowing turns first to the senses and to the experience that results from the functioning of our senses.

The senses are the windows or doorways of the mind. Whatever comes into the mind from the outside world comes into it through the senses. What comes into it may be words or sentences that other human beings utter. As everyone knows, we learn a great deal that way, certainly from the moment that our schooling begins. But learning does not begin with schooling. Nor does all our learning, even after schooling, involve statements made by others. Taking the human race as a whole, as well as human infants in every generation, learning begins with sense experience before the learners use words to express what they have learned.

In Aristotle's day, it was generally thought that we have five external senses—sight, hearing, touch, smell, and taste. The reason Aristotle called them external senses is that each involves a sense organ on the surface of our bodies, there to be acted on by the outside world: sight results from the action on our eyes of things outside us, hearing from what outside acts on our ears, touch from what outside acts on our skin, smell from what outside acts on our nose, and taste from what outside acts on our tongue and mouth.

Modern scientific research has discovered that we have more than five senses and sense organs; for example, the sense organs by which we sense hunger and thirst within our own bodies and the sense organs by which we sense the motion of our limbs or the position of our bodies. But the exact number of senses and sense organs does not affect the account that Aristotle gives of the contribution that the senses and sense experience make to our thinking and knowing.

Each of the senses produces sensations only when its sense organ is acted on physically by something in the outside world. The senses are passive receivers that must be activated from the outside. Each of our sense organs is a highly specialized receiver. We cannot taste or smell things with our eyes; we cannot hear or see them with our tongues and noses. We are aware of colors through our eyes, of sounds through our ears, of odors through our nose, and so on.

Certain aspects of the world around us we can be aware of in more than one way. The size and shape of bodies we can see as well as feel by touch. We can see and hear the motion of bodies from one place to another, and we can even tell whether that motion is slow or fast.

Sensations of the various kinds just mentioned are the raw materials out of which our sense experience is formed. Though these raw materials come in separately from outside, through the channels of different sense organs, they do not remain separate, or isolated from one another, in our sense experience. The world we experience through our senses is a world of bodies of various sizes and shapes, in motion or at rest, and related to one another in space in a variety of ways. Our experience of this world of bodies also includes a wide variety of qualities—the colors bodies have, the sounds they make, the roughness or the smoothness of their surfaces, and so on.

According to Aristotle, our sense experience is the product of perception on our part. The sensations we receive passively through our sense organs are merely the raw materials that we somehow put together to constitute the seamless fabric of our sense experience. In that putting together, we are more active than passive.

Sensation is input from the outside. But the sense experience that arises from our perception of that outside world involves memory and imagination on our part. It is composed of many elements, all having their origin in what our various senses take in, but transformed by the way they are put together to make up the whole that is the world we perceive.

If we describe any typical perceptual experience in words, we see at once that there is much more to it than the raw materials of sensation. For example, you perceive a big, black, barking dog chasing a tiger-striped, yellow cat down the street, and the cat runs in front of a blue automobile that screeches to a sudden halt. In that description of a sense experience, only a few words name visible or audible qualities sensed by the eye and the ear—the colors and the sounds. A dog and a cat, an automobile and a street, chasing, running, and suddenly slowing down to a halt—all these things that you perceive involve more than sensations received from outside.

When you perceive an object that you call a dog or a cat, or when you perceive actions that you call chasing or running, your memory and your imagination are involved, especially if the dog you perceive is a stranger to you, while the cat is a familiar animal that you have seen around before. In addition, your understanding is involved. You have some understanding of the kind of animal that a cat is, different in kind from dogs. You have some understanding of what tigers are like, as indicated by your perception of the cat as tiger striped. You understand the difference between walking and running, between going fast and slowing down. If you did not understand all these things, you could not have had the perceptual experience that was described.

According to Aristotle, these various understandings that we have result from the activity of our mind, not from the activity of our senses. Our mind forms ideas of cats and dogs, of running and chasing. Ideas are based on the information that our senses receive from the outside world, but the ideas themselves are not received from the outside world. They are, according to Aristotle, the product of the mind's activity in its effort to understand the world we experience through our senses.

Just as we can sense things because they are capable of being sensed, so we can understand things because they are understandable. If the barking dog and the screeching car were not visible and audible, we could not see and hear them. Similarly, if the dog and the cat were not understandable as different kinds of things, we could not understand them as having different natures. In Aristotle's view, we apprehend the natures of cats or dogs by our idea or understanding of what a cat is or what a dog is, just as we apprehend the blackness of the dog or the blueness of the automobile by the visual sensations received by our eyes.

When a carpenter sets out to make a chair, he must have in mind an idea of the chair he wants to make. He must not only have an idea of chairs in general but also the more definite idea of the particular chair he wishes to make. Working with these ideas and with pieces of wood as his raw material, the carpenter shapes those pieces of wood and puts them together so that they take on the form of a chair. The idea in the mind of the productive worker has become the form of the material he works on.

Living matter having a certain form is a cat. Living matter having a different form is a dog. When children learn to distinguish between cats and dogs and to recognize each when they see it, their perception of cats and dogs involves some understanding of the special nature of each of these two kinds of animals. That understanding consists in their having an idea of what a cat is and an idea of what a dog is.

In Aristotle's view, having the idea of a cat amounts to having in one's mind the form that is common to all cats and makes each cat the kind of animal it is. This leads him to say that, just as the hand is the tool of tools (the instrument by which we use other instruments), so the mind is the form of forms. Another way of saying the same thing describes the mind as the place where the forms that are in things become our ideas of them.

The mind forms ideas by taking the forms of things and separating them from the matter of things. Producing ideas is the very opposite of producing things. In producing things, we put the ideas that we have in our minds into things by transforming matter in accordance with our ideas. In producing ideas, our minds take the forms out of things and turn them into ideas whereby we understand the nature of the things that have this or that form.

Getting or producing ideas should also be contrasted with eating things. When we eat an apple, we take both its form and its matter into our bodies. The form without the matter would not nourish us. The matter without the form would not be an apple. But when we get the idea of an apple, we take the form away from the matter of the apple. The action of our mind in doing so turns the form of an apple into an idea of the kind of fruit an apple is.

The ideas or understandings so far mentioned are ideas or understandings of objects that we perceive. They are the kind of objects that are present in our sense experience. They are also the kind of objects we can remember when they are absent. They are even the kind of objects that we can imagine, as we might imagine a cat or dog that we have never perceived, or dream of one that is strangely shaped or colored.

But when the mind starts producing ideas on the basis of sense experience, it does not stop with ideas that enable us to understand objects we can perceive, remember, and imagine. We can understand many objects of thought that we cannot perceive, such as good and bad, right and wrong, freedom and justice. We could not have discussed these objects in earlier chapters of this book if we did not understand them—if we had not formed ideas of them.

Thinking begins with the formation of ideas on the basis of the information received by our senses. Sensations are the input the mind receives from the outside world. Ideas are the output the mind produces as a result of what it receives.

Thinking goes further. It relates the ideas it produces. It joins them together, separates them, and sets one idea against another. By these further activities of thinking, the mind produces knowledge, not only knowledge about objects we can perceive, remember, or imagine, but also knowledge of objects that do not fall within our sense experience. Arithmetic, algebra, and geometry are good examples of such knowledge.

A sensation is neither true nor false. You simply have it, as when you sense the blackness of a dog or the blueness of an automobile. Even when your senses deceive you, as they often do, the sensation itself is neither true nor false. The dog, for example, may have been in shadows. In bright sunlight, it would have been seen by you as gray, not black. Your sensing it as black when it is in shadows is not false; but if, on the basis of that information alone, you *think* that it *is* black, you may be in error. The error is in your thinking, not in your sensing.

Every common noun and almost every adjective and verb in our language names an object of thought—an object we can think about because we have formed an idea of it. Not all the objects we can think about are objects we can also perceive, remember, or imagine. Dogs and cats, for example, are objects that we can perceive, but we can also think about them when there are no dogs and cats around for us to perceive through our senses. In addition, we can think about the very small particles of matter inside the atom although our senses are unable to perceive anything so small, even with the help of the most powerful microscope.

Like sensations, ideas are neither true nor false. If you and I were talking to one another, and I spoke the single word "dog" or the single word "cat," you would not be able to respond by saying either yes or no. Let us assume for the moment that you and I had the same understanding of these words. What they meant for me, they also meant for you, because for each of us they expressed the same ideas. When I said "dog," you and I thought about the same object. So, too, when I said "cat."

Now suppose that when I said "cat," I nodded or pointed in the direction of an animal in the room that started to bark at that very moment. You would immediately say, "No, that is not a cat, that's a dog." My uttering the word "cat" while nodding or pointing to an animal that both of us were perceiving could have been spelled out in a sentence: "That animal over there is a cat." Your saying no could also have been spelled out by saying, "If you think that animal is a cat, you are in error. That statement you have just made is false."

We cannot be in error just thinking of cats or dogs any more than we can be in error when we see the dog standing in the shadows as black rather than gray. Only when we make some assertion, such as "That dog *is* black," does the question arise whether what we say or think is true or false. That word "is" must enter into our thinking, and along with it goes another word, "not." When "is" and "is not" enter into our thinking, we have passed from the level of just having ideas to the level of combining and separating them. Then we have reached the level where we are forming opinions that can be either true or false.

There are other words, such as "and," "if" and "then," "since" and "therefore," "either, or," "not both," that enter our thinking at a still higher level of thought. This is the level at which making one statement leads us to affirm another or to reject another as false.

Aristotle distinguishes among these three levels of thought in his account of how the mind operates to produce knowledge. From the raw materials of sense experience, the mind forms ideas. Ideas in turn are the raw materials out of which the mind forms judgments in which something is affirmed or denied. As single ideas are expressed in speech by single words or phrases, so judgments are expressed by sentences—declarative sentences in which the words "is" or "is not" occur.

The third level Aristotle calls reasoning or inference. Only when one statement becomes the basis for asserting or denying another statement does the mind move up to the third level of thought. At this level, thinking involves giving reasons for what we think. At this level, what we think may not only be either true or false, it may also be either logical or illogical.

Aristotle was a great logician. He founded the science of logic. He wrote the first book on the subject, a book that was the standard textbook for many centuries and that still exerts considerable influence. In the next chapter, we shall consider some of his basic rules for conducting our thinking in a logical manner.

Although logical thinking is better than illogical thinking, it does not always reach conclusions that are true. Aristotle pointed out that it is possible for the mind to hold opinions that are true without reaching them in a logical manner. even as it is possible for logical thinking to result in false conclusions. Hence after we pay some attention to what makes thinking logical or illogical, we shall have to consider what makes thinking true or false.

17

Logic's Little Words

As Newton's name is associated with the law of gravitation, so Aristotle's is associated with the law of contradiction. As Einstein's name is to the theory of relativity, so Aristotle's is to the theory of syllogism. Two words lie at the heart of the law of contradiction: "is" and "is not." Two pairs of words are central to the theory of the syllogism—Aristotle's account of correct and incorrect reasoning. They are "if" and "then," "since" and "therefore."

As a rule of thought, the law of contradiction tells us primarily what *not* to do. It is a law *against* contradiction, a law that commands us to *avoid* contradicting ourselves, either in our speech or in our thought. It tells us that we should not answer a question by saying both yes and no. Stated in another way, it tells us that we should not affirm and deny the same proposition. If I say or think that Plato *was* Aristotle's teacher, I should avoid saying or thinking that Plato *was not* Aristotle's teacher. To say or think that would be to deny something that I have affirmed.

You may ask why this rule of thought is so basic and so sound. Aristotle's answer is that the law of contradiction is not only a rule of thought but also a statement about the world itself—about the realities we try to think about.

The law of contradiction, as a statement about reality, says what is immediately obvious to common sense. A thing—whatever it may be—cannot both exist and not exist at the same time. It either exists or it does not exist, but not both at once. A thing cannot have a certain attribute and not have that attribute at the same time. The apple in my hand that I am looking at cannot, at this instant, be both red in color and not red in color.

This is so very obvious that Aristotle calls the law of contradiction self-evident. Its self-evidence, for him, means its undeniability. It is impossible to think that the apple is both red and not red at the same time, just as it is impossible to think that a part is greater than the whole to which it belongs. It is impossible to think that a tennis ball that you hit over the fence is to be found in the grass that lies beyond and, at the same time, to think that it cannot be found there because it no longer exists.

The law of contradiction as a statement about reality itself underlies the law of contradiction as a rule of thought. The law of contradiction as a statement about reality *describes* the way things are. The law of contradiction as a rule of thought *prescribes* the way we should think about things if we wish our thinking about them to conform to the way things are.

When a pair of statements are contradictory, both cannot be true, nor can both be false. One must be true, the other false. Plato either was or was not Aristotle's teacher. All swans are white or some are not. However, if instead of saying that some swans are not white, which contradicts the statement that all swans are white, I had said no swans are white, a contradiction would not have resulted. People who are not acquainted with Aristotle's distinction between contradictory and contrary statements may be surprised by this.

It is possible for both of these statements— "All swans are white" and "No swans are white"—to be false, though both cannot be true. Some swans may be white and some black, in which case it is false to say that all swans are white or that none is. Aristotle calls a pair of statements contrary, not contradictory, when both cannot be true, but both can be false.

Is there a pair of statements, both of which can be true, but both of which cannot be false? Yes, according to Aristotle, the statement that some swans are white and the statement that some swans are not white can both be true, but both cannot be false. Swans must be either white or not white, and so if only some are white, some must be not white. Aristotle calls this pair of statements subcontrary.

Suppose, however, that instead of saying that some swans are white and some swans are not white, I had said "Some swans are white" and "Some swans are black." Would that pair of statements have been subcontrary—impossible for both to be false? No, because some swans might be gray, or green, yellow, or blue. *White* and *black* are not exclusive alternatives. It is not true that any visible object must be either white or black.

This being the case, it will not do to pose as the contrary of "All swans are white" the statement "All swans are black," for neither may be true and both can be false. To state the contrary of "All swans are white," one must say "No swans are white," not "All swans are black."

Unlike "black" and "white," some pairs of terms, which are contrary terms, do exhaust the alternatives. For example, all integers or whole numbers are either odd or even. There is no third possibility. When one uses terms that are exclusive alternatives, it is possible to state a contradiction without using "is" and "is not." The statement that any given whole number is an odd number is contradicted by the statement that that number is an even number, because if it is odd, it is not even, and if it is even, it is not odd, and it must be one or the other.

I cannot exaggerate the importance of Aristotle's rules concerning statements that are incompatible with one another in one of these three ways—through being contradictory of one another, through being contrary to one another, or subcontrary to one another. The importance is that observing these rules not only helps us to avoid making inconsistent statements but also helps us to detect inconsistencies in the statements made by others and to challenge what they say.

When a person we are conversing with contradicts himself or herself or makes contrary statements, we have every right to stop him and say, "You cannot make both of those statements. Both cannot be true. Which of the two do you really mean? Which do you want to claim as true?"

It is particularly important to observe that general statements—statements containing the word "all"—can be contradicted by a single negative instance. To contradict the generalization that all swans are white, one needs only to point to a single swan that is not white. That single negative instance falsifies the generalization.

Scientific generalizations are put to the test in this way. The claim that they are true can be upheld only so long as no negative instances are found to falsify them. Since the search for negative instances is an unending one, a scientific generalization can never be regarded as finally or completely verified.

Human beings are prone to generalize, especially in their thinking about other human beings who differ from themselves in sex, race, or religion. If they are men, they will permit themselves to say—unthinkingly, one hopes—that all women are such and such. If they are white persons, they will permit themselves to say that all blacks are so and so. If they are Protestants, they will permit themselves to say that all Catholics are this or that. In every one of these cases, one negative instance suffices to invalidate the generalization; and the more negative instances one can point to, the easier it is to show how wild the generalization was in the first place.

The use of contrary terms, such as "black" and "white," or "odd" and "even," brings into play another set of words that control our thinking according to certain rules—"either-or" and "not both." For example, when we toss a coin to decide something, we know that when it lands, it must be either heads or tails, not both. That is a strong disjunction. There are, however, weak disjunctions, in which something may be either this or that, and perhaps both, though not in the same respect or at the same time. To say of tomatoes that they are either red or green permits us to say that one and the same tomato can be both red and green, but at different times.

Disjunctions, especially strong disjunctions, enable us to make simple, direct inferences. If we know that a whole number is not odd, we can infer immediately that it must be even. Similarly, if we know that a whole number is not a prime number, we can infer immediately that it must be divisible by numbers other than itself and one. When we see that the tossed coin has landed heads up, we know at once that we, who bet on tails, have lost the toss. We do not have to turn the coin over to be sure of that.

Inferences of this sort Aristotle calls immediate inferences because one goes immediately from the truth or falsity of one statement to the truth or falsity of another. No steps of reasoning are involved. If one knows that it is true that all swans are white, one also knows immediately that some swans are white; and in addition one knows that at least some white objects are swans.

One can make mistakes in this simple process of inference, and mistakes are frequently made. For example, from the fact that all swans are white, it is correct to infer that some white objects are swans, but quite incorrect to infer that all white objects are swans.

That incorrect inference Aristotle calls an illicit conversion. The class of white objects is larger than the class of swans. Swans are only some of the white objects in the world. To make the mistake of thinking that because all swans are white, we can also say that all white objects are swans is to treat the two classes as coextensive, which they are not.

Two pairs of words are operative in immediate inference as well as in the more complex process of reasoning. They are "if" and "then," and "since" and "therefore." In order to express the logical correctness of an immediate inference (the inference that some swans are white from the fact that all swans are white), we say, "*If* all swans are white, *then* it *must follow* that some swans are white." To express the incorrectness of an illicit conversion, we say, "*If* all swans are white, *then* it *does not follow* that all white objects are swans."

"If-then" statements of these two kinds are statements of logically correct and logically incorrect inferences. The important point to note here is that the truth of these "if-then" statements about logically correct and logically incorrect inferences does not in any way depend upon the truth of the statements connected by "if" and "then."

The statement that all swans are white may in fact be false, and it would still be logically correct to infer that some swans are white, *if*—but only *if*—all are. Even if the statement that all white objects are swans were in fact true instead of false, it would still be logically incorrect to infer that all white objects are swans from the fact that all swans are white.

So much for the use of "if" and "then"—the latter accompanied by the words "it *must* follow" or "it *does not* follow"—to express our recognition of correct and incorrect inferences. What about "since" and "therefore"? When we substitute "since" and "therefore" for "if" and "then," we are actually making the inference that we did not make when we said only "if" and "then."

To stay with the same example that we have been using, I have made no actual inferences about swans or white objects in all the "if-then" statements I have made about them. I do not make an actual inference until I say, "*Since* all swans are white, it *therefore* follows that some swans are white." My assertion that all swans are white enables me to assert that some swans are white.

Only when I make assertions of this kind, connected by "since" and "therefore," does the truth or falsity of my first statement affect the truth or falsity of my second. My inference may be logically correct, but the conclusion of my actual inference may be actually false because my initial statement, introduced by the word "since," is false in fact. The truth may be that no swans are white, and so it was false to conclude that some are, even though it was logically correct to do so.

When I say, "If all swans are white . . . ," I am only saying *if all are,* not *that all are.* But when I say "Since all swans are white . . . ," I am saying *that all are.* Should I be right in making that assertion, I would also be right in asserting that some swans are white.

What has just been said about Aristotle's rules of immediate inference helps me to summarize briefly the rules of reasoning that constitute his theory of the syllogism. Here is a model syllogism:

> *Major premise:* All animals are mortal.
> *Minor premise:* All men are animals.
> *Conclusion:* All men are mortal.

Let us consider two more examples of reasoning syllogistically—from a major and a minor premise to a conclusion. First, this one in which the reasoning is logically valid, but the conclusion is false because the minor premise is false.

> *Major premise:* Angels are neither male nor female.
> *Minor premise:* Some men are angels.
> *Conclusion:* Some men are neither male nor female.

And this one in which a true conclusion follows logically from two true premises.

> *Major premise:* Mammals do not lay eggs.
> *Minor premise:* Human beings are mammals.
> *Conclusion:* Human beings do not lay eggs.

Considering these three different pieces of reasoning, we can observe at once that syllogistic reasoning is more complicated than immediate inference. In immediate inference, we go at once from a single statement to another single statement, and both statements will have the same terms. In syllogistic reasoning, we go from two statements, in which there are three different terms, to a conclusion in which two of these three terms occur.

In the first example above, the three terms in the major and minor premise were "animals," "men," and "mortal." And the two terms in the conclusion were "men" (a term in the minor premise) and "mortal" (a term in the major premise). That is always the case in syllogistic reasoning, and it is always the case that the third term, which occurs in both premises ("animals"), has been dropped out of the conclusion.

Aristotle calls the term that is common to the major and the minor premise the middle term. It is dropped out of the conclusion because it has served its function in the reasoning process. That function is to connect the other two terms with each other. The middle term mediates between them. That is why Aristotle calls syllogistic reasoning mediated as contrasted with immediate inference. In immediate inference, there is no middle term because there is no need of mediation.

I will not bother to spell out how this works in the three examples of syllogistic reasoning just given. You can do that for yourself. The only additional rules that you must note are these. First, that if the major or the minor premise is negative (if it contains some form of "is not" instead of "is," or "no" instead of "all"), then the conclusion must also be negative. You cannot draw an affirmative conclusion if one of the premises is negative.

The second rule is that the middle term must function connectively. Here is an example in which the middle term fails to do so.

Major premise:	No men are by nature beasts of burden.
Minor premise:	No mules are by nature men.
Conclusion:	No mules are by nature beasts of burden.

Not only is the conclusion false in fact, but it is also a logically incorrect conclusion. An affirmative conclusion must be drawn from two affirmative premises, but no conclusion at all can be validly drawn from two negative premises. The reason is that the negative in the major premise excludes all men from the class of things that are by nature beasts of burden; and the negative in the minor premise excludes all mules from the class of men. Hence we cannot correctly infer anything at all about the relation between the class of mules and the class of things that are by nature beasts of burden.

It is interesting to observe in the example just given that the major and minor premises are both true, while the conclusion that does not logically follow from them is false. It is quite possible for both premises to be false in fact and for a false conclusion to follow logically from them. For example:

Major premise: No fathers have daughters.
Minor premise: All married men are fathers.
Conclusion: No married men have daughters.

What all these examples (and many others that we might consider) show us is something that has already been pointed out and is, perhaps, worth repeating. Reasoning may be logically correct regardless of whether the premises and the conclusion are true or false in fact. Only if both premises are in fact true is the conclusion that follows logically from them also in fact true.

If either premise is false, then the conclusion that follows logically from them may be either true or false. We cannot tell which it is. On the other hand, if the conclusion that follows logically from certain premises is in fact false, then we can infer that one *or* both of the premises from which it is drawn must also be false.

This leads us to one more important rule of reasoning that Aristotle pointed out. In syllogistic reasoning, as in immediate inference, the validity of the inference is expressed by an "if" and a "then." In the case of syllogistic reasoning, we are saying that *if* the two premises are true, *then* the conclusion that logically follows from them is also true. We have not yet asserted the truth of the premises. We have asserted only the validity of the inference from the premises to the conclusion. Only when we assert the truth of the premises by substituting "since" for "if," can we also substitute "therefore" for "then" and assert the truth of the conclusion.

The rule with which we are here concerned has two parts. On the one hand, it says that we have a right to assert the truth of the conclusion if we assert the truth of the premises. On the other hand, it says that we have a right to question the truth of the premises if we deny the truth of the conclusion. I say "question the truth of the premises" rather than "deny the truth of the premises" because when we deny the truth of the conclusion, we know only that either one of the premises is false or that both may be, but we do not know which is the case.

The double-edged rule just stated is particularly applicable to a kind of reasoning that Aristotle called hypothetical. It usually involves four terms, not three.

Alexander Hamilton, in one of the *Federalist* papers, said: "If men were angels, no government would be necessary." If, having said that, Hamilton went on to deny that men were angels, no conclusion would follow. Denying the *if* statement (which is called the antecedent in hypothetical reasoning) does not entitle you to deny the *then* statement (which is called the consequent).

However, Hamilton obviously thought that government is unquestionably necessary for a society of human beings. He would, therefore, have had no hesitation in denying that men are angels. He would have been right in doing so because denying the consequent (or the *then* statement) in hypothetical reasoning does entitle you to deny the antecedent (or the *if* statement).

The truth that Hamilton is getting at can also be expressed in a single complex statement that conceals rather than reveals the reasoning behind it. That complex statement is as follows: "Because men are not angels, government is necessary for human society." The reasoning that goes unexpressed involves a series of statements about the difference between men and angels as well as statements about the special characteristics of men that make government necessary for human society. The kind of compressed argument that omits or conceals indispensable premises Aristotle called an enthymeme.

18

Telling the Truth and Thinking It

The word "truth" has been used over and over again in the two preceding chapters. Since those chapters are about the way the mind works and about thinking and knowing, it is quite natural that reference to truth and falsity should have been frequent. When we know something, what we know is the truth about it. When we try to think correctly and soundly, our effort is to get at the truth.

I thought it possible to use the words "truth" and "falsity" (or "true" and "false") without explaining what they mean because everyone does understand what they mean. They are common notions, commonly used. The question "What is truth?" is not a difficult question to answer. After you understand what truth is, the difficult question, as we shall see, is: How can we tell whether a particular statement is true or false?

The reason why I say that everyone, as a matter of common sense, understands truth and falsity is that everyone knows how to tell a lie. Every one of us has told lies on one occasion or another, and everyone understands the difference between telling a lie and telling the truth.

Let us suppose that I think a certain restaurant is closed on Sunday. On a Sunday morning, you ask me whether that restaurant is open for dinner that evening. I tell you that it is. For the moment, let us not be concerned with the reason why I lied to you. My lying consisted in saying in words the very opposite of what I think. I said that a certain restaurant *is* open for dinner when at the same time I think it is *not* open.

To say "is" when you think "is not"—or to say "is not" when you think "is"—is to tell a lie. To tell the truth is the very opposite of this. It consists in saying "is" when you think "is," and "is not" when you think "is not."

An American philosopher who taught at Harvard University at the beginning of this century wittily remarked that a liar is a person who willfully misplaces his ontological predicates. "Is" and "is not" are what he meant by ontological predicates. A liar, in other words, is a person who intentionally puts "is" in place of "is not," or "is not" in place of "is." To tell the truth then, is to have what one says in words agree with or conform to what one thinks. To lie is not to say in words what one thinks, but the very opposite of it.

As I said a moment ago, everyone understands this. All I have done is to spell out, as explicitly as possible, what everyone understands. I have done so as preparation for Aristotle's simple, clear, and commonsense answer to the question about what makes our thinking true or false.

His answer is that, just as telling the truth to another person consists in an agreement between what one says and what one thinks, so thinking truly consists in an agreement between what one thinks and what one is thinking about. For example, if I am asked whether Christopher Columbus was a Spaniard or an Italian, I think truly if I think he was an Italian and falsely if I think he was not an Italian.

This one example suffices for an understanding of Aristotle's explanation of what makes our thinking true or false. We think truly (or have truth in our mind) if we think that that which is, is; or that that which is not, is not. We think falsely (or have falsity in our mind) if we think that that which is, is not; or that that which is not, is.

In the case of telling the truth to someone else, the agreement is between what we say in words to another person and what we actually think. In the case of thinking the truth, the agreement is between what we think and the facts as they are. Truth consists in a correspondence between the mind and reality.

We express most of our thoughts in words, whether we are speaking to ourselves or to someone else or writing our thoughts down in some fashion. Not all the thoughts we express orally are either true or false. Aristotle points out that questions are neither true nor false; nor are the requests we make of others, nor the commands we give. Only declarative sentences—sentences that contain some form of the words "is" and "is not," or that can be rephrased to contain those words—are true or false.

This should not seem surprising in view of the fact that Aristotle's understanding of what makes a statement true lies in its agreement with the facts of the matter. Declarative statements are the only statements that try to describe the facts—the way things are. Only such statements can either succeed in doing so or fail to do so. If they succeed, they are true; if they fail, they are false.

It would appear, then, that statements that are *prescriptive* rather than *descriptive* cannot be either true or false. A prescriptive statement is one that prescribes what you or I ought to do. How can a statement that says that I ought to devote more time to reading books and less to playing games be true or false if truth and falsity in the statement of our thoughts consist in an agreement between what we assert or deny and the way things are or are not?

Being able to answer that question is of great importance. If there were no answer to it, statements about the goals we ought to aim at in life, and about the means we ought to employ in order to reach them, would be neither true nor false.

Everything we learned from Aristotle about the pursuit of happiness (in Part III of this book) might still be interesting as an expression of Aristotle's opinions about such matters. But he could not claim, and I could not claim, truth for his recommendations about what we ought to do in order to achieve the good human life that we are under a moral obligation to try to achieve.

Aristotle obviously thought that his teaching about the good life and how to achieve it was true. Therefore, he must have had an answer to the question about the truth of statements that contain the words "ought" or "ought not." He did. He said that, just as a *descriptive* statement is true if it agrees with or conforms to reality, so a *prescriptive* statement is true if it agrees with or conforms to right desire.

What is right desire? It consists in desiring what one ought to desire. What ought one to desire? Whatever is really good for a human being. What is really good for a human being? Whatever satisfies a human need.

The statement that a person ought to desire whatever is really good for himself or herself is a self-evident truth. It is self-evident in the same way that the statement that a part is less than the finite whole to which it belongs is self-evidently true. Just as it is impossible for us to think of a part that is greater than the whole to which it belongs, or of a whole that is less than any of its parts, so it is impossible for us to think that we *ought not* to desire that which is *really good* for us, or that we *ought* to desire that which is *really bad* for us.

Among our human needs is the need for knowledge. Knowledge is really good for human beings to have. Since right desire consists in desiring what we ought to desire, the statement that we ought to desire knowledge conforms to right desire. Because it conforms to right desire, it is true, according to Aristotle's theory of what makes a prescriptive statement true.

We have just taken the easiest step toward answering the question about how we can tell whether a statement is true or false. A statement such as "A finite whole is greater than any of its parts" reveals its truth on its very face. As soon as we understand the terms that make up the statement—"whole," "part," and "greater than"—we immediately see that the statement is true. It is impossible to understand what a whole is, what a part is, and the relation of *greater than,* without at the same time understanding a whole to be greater than any of its parts.

There are not many statements we can make that are self-evidently true in this way. The statement that what is really good ought to be desired is one of them. But its truth is not as manifest as the truth about wholes and parts because it is easier for us to understand wholes and parts than it is to understand the distinction between real and apparent goods and the distinction between what ought to be desired and what is in fact desired.

We sometimes call statements self-evident that are not self-evident. When we do so, we usually wish to recommend them as generally acceptable truths—acceptable without any further argument. That is what Thomas Jefferson did when he wrote, in the Declaration of Independence, that "we hold these truths to be self-evident: that all men are created equal, that they are endowed by their Creator with certain unalienable rights," and so on. These statements may have been accepted as true by the signers of the Declaration and by others, but a fairly extended argument would have been necessary to establish their truth.

What I have just said indicates another way in which we can tell whether a statement is true or false. If it is not self-evidently true, its truth may be established by argument or reasoning. According to Aristotle, the truth of some statements can be demonstrated in this way. Two conditions are required for the demonstration or proof of a statement's truth. One is the truth of the premises used in the reasoning. The other is the correctness or validity of the reasoning itself.

Let the statement be: "The United States is larger than the State of New York." Two premises are needed to establish its truth. One is: "A whole is larger than any of its parts." The other is: "The United States is a whole, of which the State of New York is one part." From these two statements, it follows that the United States is larger than the State of New York. The premises being true, the conclusion that follows from them is also true.

Just as very few statements can be seen by us to be self-evidently true, so also very few can be seen by us to be true as a result of valid reasoning from true premises. The truth of most of the statements that express what we think is not so easily determined. In most cases, we remain in doubt about whether a statement is true or false. When we are able to resolve our doubts, we do so by appealing to the evidence afforded us by the experience of our senses.

For example, if we are in doubt whether a certain building is twelve or fifteen stories tall, the way to remove that doubt is to look at the building and count its stories. A single, relatively simple observation will tell us whether a statement about the building's height is true or false.

The appeal to observation is the way to determine the truth of statements about things that are perceivable through our senses. You may ask whether we can trust our senses. Not always, but the way to check our own observation is to have it confirmed or corroborated by the observation of others.

For example, as a result of my own observation, I may make the statement that the automobile that crashed into the wall was going very fast. Other witnesses of the same event may have to be appealed to in order to get at the truth of this matter. If all of them report the same observation, it is probably true that the automobile was going very fast when it crashed. The more witnesses who agree on this point, the more probable it is.

A statement that is only probably true has the same truth that is possessed by a statement that we regard as certainly true. Either the auto was going very fast or it was not. A statement about its speed is either true or false. When we say that a statement is only probably true, we are not estimating the degree of its truth. We are assessing our own degree of assurance in claiming truth for it.

Degrees of probability are not measures of the truth of a statement, but only measures of the assurance with which we can determine its truth. A truth that we affirm with certitude, such as the truth about wholes and parts, is no more true than a truth that we regard as only probable, such as the truth about the speed of the auto that crashed.

Some witnesses are qualified to make observations that help us to determine the truth of statements; some are not. For example, as a result of my own observation, I may say that the ring on your finger is gold. It may, of course, look as if it were gold and still be only gold plated. It is difficult, if not impossible, to tell which it is by unaided observation. Even an experienced jeweler would not give you an opinion about this just by looking at or handling the ring. The jeweler knows there are ways of determining the real character of objects that look as if they are made of gold. By putting your ring to the appropriate test and by observing the result of it, the jeweler, as an expert witness, can say whether my original statement about the ring is true or false.

So far we have considered statements about particular objects—statements about the height of a certain building, about the speed of a certain automobile, about the metal of a certain ring. The truth of such statements can be checked by observation. Sometimes, as a result of observation, our own or the observation of others as well, we can be relatively sure about the truth of the statement under consideration; sometimes, we are left unsure.

Observation seldom gives us the certainty we have about the truth of statements that are self-evidently true or that can be established as true by valid reasoning. I say "seldom" rather than "never" because, according to Aristotle, some simple statements about observable objects are as evidently true as some general statements are self-evidently true. That there is a piece of paper in my typewriter as I am writing this sentence is immediately evident to me. I do not need the confirmation of other witnesses to assure me of the truth of my statement about this observable fact. I am as certain of its truth as I am of the truth of the statement about wholes and parts.

We are left with a large class of statements that we call generalizations from experience, such statements as "All swans are white" or "All Eskimos are short." Since it is impossible for us or anyone else to observe the color of *all* swans, or the height of *all* Eskimos, observation by itself cannot establish the truth of these generalizations.

A number of observations may persuade us that the generalizations are probably true. The larger the number of observations, the more we may be persuaded. Increasing their number can only increase the probability. It can never result in certainty that the generalizations are true.

However, we can be certain that a generalization is false, even if we can never be certain that it is true. I pointed out in the preceding chapter that the statement "Some swans are black" or even the statement "This swan that I am observing is black" contradicts the statement "All swans are white." Contradictory statements cannot both be true. The truth of my observation that this one swan is black falsifies the generalization that all swans are white. In the light of that one observation, I know with certitude that the generalization is false.

Aristotle's answer to the question about how we are able to tell whether a statement is true or false can be summarized by saying that we are able to do so by appealing to experience, on the one hand, and to reason, on the other hand. Sense perception provides us with one way of checking the truth or falsity of statements in question. In addition, Aristotle recommends that we always consider the opinions of others before making up our own minds—the opinions held by most men, or by the few who are experts, or by the wise.

19

Beyond a
Reasonable Doubt

In our courts two standards are set for the verdict to be rendered by a jury. On questions of fact that the court submits to the jury, the jury is sometimes required to give an answer that it holds beyond a reasonable doubt; and sometimes it is sufficient if the jury's answer is one that it thinks is supported by a preponderance of the evidence.

Aristotle made a somewhat similar distinction between two ways in which we can answer questions of all sorts. Like the jury's answer that is beyond a reasonable doubt, we sometimes can answer a question by a statement that has the status of knowledge. When our answers do not consist of knowledge, Aristotle calls them opinions. Opinions approach knowledge to the extent that they have the weight of the evidence on their side. At the very opposite end of the scale are those opinions that are totally unsupported by evidence.

Aristotle's distinction between knowledge and opinion is a very sharp one—too sharp, perhaps, for us to accept without qualification. For him, when we have

147

knowledge, what we know consists of necessary truths. We affirm such truths with certitude because they are beyond all reasonable doubt. For example, we cannot doubt that a finite whole is greater than any of its parts. If something is a finite whole, it must be greater than any of its parts. It is impossible for it not to be.

Such self-evident truths constitute one example of what Aristotle means by knowledge. The other example consists of conclusions that can be validly demonstrated by premises that are self-evidently true. When we affirm such conclusions, we not only know *that* what they assert is true, but we also know *why* what they assert is true. Knowing the reasons why what they assert is true, we know that what they assert cannot be otherwise. Here, too, we are in possession of necessary truths.

Aristotle in his day thought that mathematics, especially geometry, exemplified knowledge of this high quality. The view that is held of mathematics in our day does not agree with Aristotle's. Nevertheless mathematics comes nearer than any other science to exemplifying what Aristotle meant by knowledge.

Considering the truths of geometry, we can understand one other distinction that Aristotle made between knowledge and opinion. There are two ways, he says, in which one can affirm the conclusion of a geometrical demonstration. The teacher who understands the demonstration affirms the conclusion in the light of the premises that prove it. He or she has knowledge. In contrast, the student who does not understand the demonstration but who affirms the conclusion only because the teacher said it is true does not have knowledge. Even if the truth itself is a necessary truth, to affirm it on the authority of someone else is to hold it as a matter of opinion rather than as knowledge. For most of us, the scientific truths with which we are acquainted are opinions we hold on the authority of scientists, not knowledge that we ourselves possess.

We may find this way of distinguishing between knowledge and opinion more useful as well as more acceptable. Only a very few statements are necessary truths for us because they are self-evidently true, and their opposites are impossible. All other statements express opinions that may or may not be true. Though Aristotle would call all statements of this sort statements of opinion rather than of knowledge, let us see whether we can divide opinions into two groups, one of which has some resemblance to what Aristotle meant by knowledge.

The opinions we hold may either be supported by reasons and by observations, or they may be held by us without such support. For example, if I hold an opinion only because someone else told me it was true, and I myself do not have any other reason for thinking it to be true, then that is a *mere* opinion on my part. The statement may in fact be true. That does not make it any the less a mere opinion. So far as affirming it is concerned, I have no grounds that provide me with reasons for thinking it to be true apart from the authority of someone else.

Each of us also has a number of personal prejudices—things we hold to be true simply because we want to believe them. We have no rational grounds for believing them. Instead, we are emotionally attached to them. For example, persons often believe that their country is the best country in the world. That may or may not be true. It may even be possible to argue that it is true by citing evidence of one sort or another or by giving reasons for thinking so. But persons who believe this usually do not cite evidence or give reasons. They just wish to believe it.

The statements to which one is emotionally attached by such wishful thinking are mere opinions. Other persons may be emotionally attached to opinions that are opposite. Since neither one opinion nor the other, which may be its very opposite, is supported by reasons or evidence, one opinion of this sort is as good as another.

In the case of mere opinions, everyone is entitled to prefer his or her own—those to which the individual is emotionally attached. About such opinions there can be no argument, at least none that is rational. Opinions of this sort are like expressions of personal taste in food or drink. You may like orange juice better than pineapple juice, and I may prefer pineapple juice to orange juice. You are entitled to your likes, and I to mine. There is no point in our arguing about which is better.

Differences of opinion become arguable only when the opinions about which we differ are not mere opinions in the sense just indicated—only when they are not simply personal prejudices, expressions of taste, or things that we wish to believe.

For example, I may have good reasons for thinking that harnessing the energy of the sun will provide us with sufficient energy when we run out of fossil fuels such as coal and oil. You may have good reasons for thinking that solar energy will not solve the problem. Each of us, in addition, may be able to cite statistics provided by careful studies of energy sources. Neither of us may be able to persuade the other. Nevertheless, the opinions we hold and about which we differ and argue are *not* mere opinions on our part.

Let us suppose that neither of us has studied the energy problem ourselves. We have simply read what has been said by others on the subject. The opposite opinions we hold are based on the authority of others. Let us further suppose that you have most of the authorities in this field on your side; or that of the authorities that can be appealed to, you have the most expert on your side. Aristotle would say that you have the stronger case. In his view, the opinion that is held either by most men, or by most of those who are experts, or by the best-qualified among the experts, is likely to turn out to be the better opinion to hold.

We approach nearer to what Aristotle meant by knowledge, and we move further away from mere opinion, when the opinions held are based on scientific evidence and scientific reasoning. Those opinions that are supported by a preponderance of the evidence and by the soundest reasoning are regarded by scientists in our day as knowledge.

It is not knowledge in Aristotle's sense of the term because what we claim to know may turn out not to be the better of two opposite opinions when, by further scientific investigation, more evidence is found on the opposite side; or when, by further scientific thought, better reasons are found for holding the opposite opinion. No scientific conclusion is known by us to be finally or ultimately true—true beyond the possibility of correction or rejection by further investigation and further thought about the matter.

The opposite of any opinion that we hold as a scientific conclusion always remains possible because no scientific conclusion is itself a necessary truth. Nevertheless, a large number of scientific conclusions have been supported by a preponderance of the evidence and by unchallenged reasons for many centuries. The fact that new discoveries may shift the scales against these conclusions or the fact that the reasons in favor of them may be seriously challenged by new thinking about the subject does not prevent us from regarding such conclusions as well-established knowledge—*for the time being*.

Are scientific conclusions, supported by a preponderance of the evidence and by the best reasoning that is available at the time, the only opinions we are entitled to regard as knowledge? No. Philosophical conclusions may also be opinions that we are entitled to regard as knowledge because they are supported by sound reasoning and by the weight of the evidence that is in favor of them rather than their opposites.

How do the conclusions of philosophical thought differ from the conclusions of scientific research? The answer lies in the two words "thought" and "research." Scientific conclusions are based on the investigations undertaken by scientists, whether in laboratories or not. The thinking that scientists do to reach these conclusions never by itself suffices. It is always thinking about the observations or findings of carefully planned and carefully executed research or investigation.

In contrast, philosophical thought reaches conclusions based on common experience, the kind of experience that all of us have every day of our lives without doing any research—without carefully carrying out carefully planned investigations. Philosophers do no research. They do not devise experiments or carry out investigations.

Philosophical thought about common experience begins with the common-sense opinions that most persons hold. It improves upon such common-sense opinions by being more reflective and analytical than most persons are. In my own view of the matter, it reaches its best and most-refined conclusions in what I have called Aristotle's uncommon common sense.

Scientific or philosophical conclusions are usually generalizations from experience—either the special experience that results from research or investigation or the common experience that all of us have without investigation or research. As we noted in an earlier chapter, any generalization can be falsified by a single negative observation. This is as true of a philosophical as it is of a scientific generalization. The longer a generalization goes without being falsified, the more entitled we are to regard it as established knowledge even though we can never regard it as finally or ultimately true—beyond the possibility of correction or rejection.

Because philosophical conclusions are based on common rather than on special experience, because they are not affected by the results of investigation or research, conclusions of the kind that Aristotle reached more than two thousand years ago can still claim the status of philosophical knowledge in our day. Nothing in our common experience since his time has falsified them.

Most of the scientific conclusions that were currently accepted in Aristotle's day have been rejected or corrected since then. They have either been falsified by the discoveries of later research, or they have been corrected and improved by better thinking as well as by better observations and more thorough investigations.

Not all opinions that can be regarded as established knowledge take the form of scientific or philosophical generalizations from experience. Historical investigation or research reaches conclusions about particular matters of fact—the date when some event took place, the steps by which some individual became a ruler, the circumstances that led to the outbreak of a war, and so forth.

Here, as in the case of science, research amasses evidence about which historians think and, in the light of their thinking, advance conclusions that they regard as supported by a preponderance of the evidence and by good reasons. When they are reached in this way, historical conclusions can be regarded as established knowledge even though further research may change our view of the matter.

We now see that there are at least five different kinds of knowledge, only one of which is knowledge in the strict sense that Aristotle attaches to that word. That one is the knowledge we have when we understand truths that are self-evident. The other four kinds are (1) the well-founded opinions of mathematical thought—the conclusions that mathematicians are able to demonstrate; (2) the well-established generalizations of scientific research or investigation; (3) the philosophical opinions that are based on common experience and on the refinement of common sense by philosophical reflection; and (4) the opinions about particular facts that historians are able to support by historical research.

All four are opinions in the sense that they are never so firmly established by reasons and evidence that they cannot be falsified or corrected by further thought or new observations. Yet all four are also knowledge in the sense that at a given time they have the weight of the evidence in their favor and the reasoning that supports them remains unchallenged.

PART V

DIFFICULT
PHILOSOPHICAL
QUESTIONS

20

Infinity

Difficult philosophical questions are questions that it is impossible to answer in the light of common experience and by the use of common sense. To answer them requires sustained reflection and reasoning.

How do such questions arise? For Aristotle they arose in part from the refinements of common sense that his own philosophical thought developed. In part, they were questions he asked in response to the views of others that were current in his day.

Among the students of nature who preceded him were two Greek physicists, Leucippus and Democritus, who first proposed the theory of atoms. According to their theory, everything in the world of nature is composed of tiny, invisible particles of matter, separated by a void—space totally devoid of matter. They called these particles atoms to indicate that these units of matter were not merely very small, but absolutely small. Nothing smaller, in their view, can exist, for each atom is an indivisible unit of matter. It cannot be cut up into smaller units.

Atoms, according to Democritus, differ from one another only in size, shape, and weight. They are constantly in motion. And they are infinite in number.

Confronted with this theory, Aristotle raised two objections to it. In the first place, he challenged the central notion in the theory of atomism. If an atom is a solid unit of matter with no void or empty space inside it, then, he argued, it cannot be uncuttable or indivisible. Either an atom has some empty space inside it, in which case it is not a unit of matter; or, lacking empty space, the matter is continuous, in which case it is divisible.

The reasoning here can be illustrated by taking something larger than an atom. I am holding in my hand one matchstick. I break it into two smaller pieces of wood. Each of these pieces of wood is now a separate unit of matter. No longer being one piece of wood, they can no longer be broken into two. But each of the two pieces of wood can be further divided, and so on without end.

Whatever is continuous, Aristotle held, is infinitely divisible. Anything that is one—a single unit of matter—must be continuous. If it were not, it would not be one unit of matter, but two or more. By this reasoning, Aristotle thought he showed that there could be no atoms. There may be very small units of matter, but however small these particles may be, they can be divided into smaller particles, if each is a unit of matter—one and continuous.

In the second place, Aristotle objected to the view that there are an infinite number of atoms in the world. The number may be very large, so large that it cannot be counted in any time that a counter might use to do so. But it cannot be an infinite number because, Aristotle maintained, an infinite number of things cannot actually coexist at any moment of time.

These two objections that Aristotle raised against the atomists of his day may at first appear to be inconsistent. On the one hand, Aristotle appears to be saying that any continuous unit of matter must be infinitely divisible. On the other hand, he appears to be saying that there cannot be an infinite number of units in existence at any one time. Is he not both affirming the existence of an infinity and also denying it?

The apparent contradiction is resolved by a distinction that is characteristic of Aristotle's thought. We have come upon this distinction in an earlier chapter of this book (see chapter 7). It is the distinction between the potential and the actual—between what can be (but is not) and what is.

Aristotle thinks that there can be two infinities—both potential, neither actual. One is the potential infinite of addition. The other is the potential infinite of division.

The potential infinite of addition is exemplified in the infinity of whole numbers. There is no whole number that is the last number in the series of whole numbers from one, two, three, four, and so on. Given any number in that series, however large it may be, there is a next one that is larger. It is possible to go on adding number after number without end. But it is only *possible,* you cannot *actually* carry out this process of addition, for to do so would take an infinite time—time without end.

Aristotle, as we shall see in the next chapter, did not deny the infinity of time. On the contrary, he affirmed the eternity of the world—that it has no beginning or end. But an infinite time does not exist at any one moment. Like the infinite series of whole numbers, it is only a potential, not an actual, infinite.

So, too, the infinity of division is a potential, not an actual, infinite. Just as you can go on adding number after number without end, so you can go on dividing anything that is continuous without end. The number of fractions between the whole numbers two and three is infinite, just as the number of whole numbers is infinite. Both infinities, however, are potential, not actual. They do not actually exist at any moment of time.

At this or any other moment, Aristotle maintained, there cannot be an actual infinity of coexisting things, as there would be if the atomists were correct in their view. They held, it must be remembered, that at this very moment an actually infinite number of atoms coexist. It is that and that alone which Aristotle denied.

His reasoning on this score ran as follows. Either the number of actually coexisting things is definite or indefinite. If it is infinite, it is indefinite. But nothing can be both actual and indefinite. Therefore, there cannot be an actual infinity of any sort—an actually infinite number of coexisting atoms, an actually infinite world, an actually infinite space that is filled with actually existing units of matter.

The only infinities that there can be, according to Aristotle, are the potential infinities that are involved in the endless processes of addition or division. Since one moment of time succeeds another or precedes another, and since two moments of time do not actually coexist, time can be infinite.

21

Eternity

Time can be infinite, Aristotle thought, because it is made up of a series of moments or instants that precede or succeed one another and do not actually coexist. One moment of time ceases to exist as the next moment of time comes into existence. Since that process can go on endlessly, there can be an infinite number of moments or instants of time.

Time can be infinite, but is it? If it is, then the world that now exists has no end. Even if it had a beginning, it can go on without end, for there is no end to time. There can always be another moment.

Aristotle went further. He not only thought that time is endless, but he also thought that the world had no beginning as well as no end. If the world had neither beginning nor end, then time is infinite in both directions. There is no moment of time that is not preceded by an earlier moment. There is no moment of time that is not succeeded by a later moment.

Why did Aristotle think the world is eternal? He used the word "eternal" to express his understanding that the world has neither beginning nor end. Sometimes the word "eternal" is used to signify *timelessness,* as when it is said that God is eternal. Aristotle used the word "eternal" in that sense, too. But, in his view, the eternity of the world is one thing, and the eternity of God quite another.

To understand this distinction between the two eternities—the eternity of timelessness and the eternity of time without beginning or end—we must consider Aristotle's understanding of time itself.

Time, he said, is the measure of motion or change. Another way of expressing this thought is to say that time is the dimension in which motion or change occurs, just as space is the dimension in which material things exist. Existing things occupy or fill space. Changing things endure in time. The billiard ball that rolls from one side of the table to the other does so in a period of time. That motion takes time. The duration of the motion is measured by the number of moments of time that it took for the billiard ball to get from here to there.

It follows, Aristotle thought, that time has neither beginning nor end if motion or change has neither beginning nor end. But why did he think that motion or change cannot begin and cannot end? That is a very difficult question, indeed.

The answer, if there is an answer, lies in Aristotle's notion of cause and effect and in his notion of God. Anything that happens, Aristotle said, must have a cause. If a body moves, something must cause it to move. That which causes a body to move must itself move. For example, the billiard ball did not move itself. It was moved by the billiard cue that struck it. To set the billiard ball in motion, the billiard cue itself had to move. But something else had to move it. And so on.

What this amounts to is a denial on Aristotle's part of a first mover in the series of movers and things moved. Aristotle, as we shall see, did affirm the existence—more than that, the necessary existence—of a first mover. But, in his view, the first mover did not come first in a series of things moving and moved. The first mover was not the first efficient cause of motion—the mover that started things moving.

In chapter 23 on God, we shall return to Aristotle's conception of the first mover. For the present, I need only point out that Aristotle's God, unlike the God of the Bible, did not create the world. Aristotle would have denied the statement with which the Bible opens: "In the beginning God created the heavens and the earth." He would have denied it because he saw no reason whatsoever for thinking that the world ever had a beginning.

If there is no reason for thinking that the world in motion ever had a beginning, there is equally no reason for thinking that the world in motion will ever come to an end. The individual things of which the world is composed come into existence and pass away. There cannot be an infinite number of individual things coexisting at any one time. But there can be an infinite number of things coming into being and passing away in an infinite time, or time without beginning or end. Coming into being and passing away is, as we have seen, one type of change. Like local motion, or movement from one place to another, it never started and it never ends.

The type of motion that Aristotle had most in mind when he talked about the eternity of motion was not the movement of bodies on earth nor any other terrestrial change. He looked up at the heavens and at the movement there of the sun and moon, the planets, and the stars. These motions, he thought, most clearly exemplified the eternity of motion and, with it, the eternity of the world. As we shall see in chapter 23, the eternity of God is used by Aristotle to explain the eternity of the world. These two eternities are as different as timelessness is different from everlasting time.

22

The Immateriality
of Mind

The three philosophical questions with which we are concerned in this chapter are not all equally difficult. The first and least difficult question is whether the material things of the physical world are also immaterial in some respect. More difficult is the question whether the existence of the human mind introduces an element of immateriality into a world that is otherwise material. Finally, and most difficult of all, is the question whether the universe includes a being or beings wholly immaterial.

The reader who remembers what was said in chapter 8 will have some clue to the answer that Aristotle gave to the first question. We saw there that all the changing things of physical nature are composed of matter and form. We understood this in terms of works of human art. The artist or craftsman takes materials that can be formed in one way or another and produces a work of art by transforming the materials he works on—giving them a form they did not originally have. The wood that becomes a chair as a result of human productivity takes on a form—the form of

164

chairness—that it did not have before the maker transformed it.

It is important to remember that we understood that form is *not* shape. The chairs that men produce have many different shapes, but whatever shape they have, they are all chairs. It is the form, not the shape, that makes all chairs of different shapes the same kind of thing. That form was an idea in the mind of the maker before it became the form by which he transformed the wood into a chair. Having that idea, the maker understood the kind of material thing he wished to make. As the idea in the mind of the maker is an understanding of the kind of thing to be made, so the form in the materials transformed by the maker is what makes it the kind of thing that is made.

Whether they are products of human art or natural rather than artificial things, all material things have an aspect that is not material. Form is not matter; matter is not form. Things composed of form and matter have an immaterial as well as a material aspect.

As we have seen, we may be able to think about matter without form, but pure matter—totally unformed matter—cannot exist. The forms that matter can take actualize its potentialities. Lacking all form, matter by itself can have no actuality; and what has no actuality does not exist.

Is it equally true to say that the forms that matter takes do not exist apart from the matter to which they give some kind of actuality—the actuality of a chair or the actuality of a tree? The forms that are the immaterial aspect of material things are material forms—forms that have their existence in matter. But is that the only existence they have? Can they also exist apart from the matter of things that are composed of matter and form?

Aristotle's answer to that question is affirmative. Once more it is necessary to remember something said in an earlier chapter. In chapter 16, I pointed out that, according to Aristotle, the human mind understands the kind of thing that a chair or a tree is by having an idea of it. Having an idea consists in having in the mind the form of the thing without having the matter of it also.

The point just made relates to the difference between mind in its activity as knower and mind in its activity as producer.

As producer, the mind has a productive idea that it uses to transform raw materials into chairs and tables. It puts its ideas into those raw materials and gives them the form of a chair or a table. As a knower, the mind gets ideas from the natural things of the physical world. It gets them by taking the forms of material things away from the matter of those composite objects—trees or horses. By doing so, it understands the kind of thing a tree or a horse is.

Another point to remember from chapter 16 is the difference between knowing and eating. When we eat (take food into our system and digest it), we take both the matter and the form of the composite thing that gives us nourishment—an apple or a potato.

As Aristotle saw it, the reason why the apple or potato that we eat gives us nourishment is that when we digest and assimilate it, we transform its matter.

Nourishment involves the assimilation of the food we eat. Assimilation occurs when matter that had the form of an apple or a potato loses that form and takes on the form of human flesh, bone, and blood. That is why we must take into our own bodies both the matter and the form of the material things from which we seek nourishment.

If knowing were exactly like eating, we would never be able to understand the kind of thing an apple or a potato is. To understand the kind of thing an apple or a potato is, we must take the forms of those composite things away from the matter that they form.

In assimilating edible things, we must separate the matter from the form and replace the form the matter had by the form of our own bodies.

In understanding knowable things, we must separate the form from the matter and keep the form separate from matter. Only as separate from matter does the form become an idea in our minds, an idea by which we understand the kind of thing an apple or a potato is.

Why? This is the difficult question that remains to be answered. Aristotle's answer turns on a distinction between the kind of thing a potato or an apple is in general, and particular potatoes or apples, each a unique thing. This particular apple that I have in my hand is the unique thing it is because the form, which makes it *an apple,* is united with this unit of matter that makes it *this apple,* not that one over there on the table. That one over there has the same form in a different unit of matter. The different units of matter that enter into the composition of two individual apples is what makes them different individuals. The form that each of them has is what makes them both apples—the same kind of fruit.

When we have the idea that enables us to understand the kind of thing an apple is, we are understanding apples in general, not this or that individual apple. In Aristotle's view, we can perceive through our senses the individuality of this or that apple, but we cannot, through the ideas we have in our minds, understand its individuality. Only kinds in general are understandable, not individuals.

That is why the mind, in its understanding of kinds in general, must separate the forms of material things from their matter and keep those forms separate as the ideas by which we understand. That is also why Aristotle called the mind the form of forms—the place where the forms of material things can exist apart from their matter.

We have now reached Aristotle's answer to the second question stated at the beginning of this chapter. Does the human mind introduce an element of immateriality into a world that is otherwise material? Yes, Aristotle said, it does.

If the mind were not an immaterial element in the makeup of human beings, it would not give us the ability to understand material things by separating their forms from their matter. And if the mind did not keep or hold the forms of material things separate from their matter, we would not have the ideas by which we understand kinds in general—the kind of thing a potato is as distinct from the kind of thing an apple is.

To keep or hold forms separate from matter, the mind itself must be immaterial. If it were material, the forms would be kept or held in matter, and then they would no longer be ideas by which we understand kinds in general.

There is another way of saying the same thing that may help us to understand Aristotle's argument a little better. Sensing and perceiving are one mode of knowing. When we sense and perceive individual things (this or that apple), such knowing involves the action of our sense organs and our brains, which are material elements in our makeup.

Understanding is a different mode of knowing. By sensing and perceiving, we know this or that individual thing. By understanding, we know the kind of thing in general that this individual thing is. Unlike sensing and perceiving, such knowing does not involve the action of any material organ, not even the brain.

Seeing is an act of the eye, but understanding is not an act of our brain. It is an act of our mind—an immaterial element in our makeup that may be related to, but is distinct from, the brain as a material organ.

To sum up what we have learned so far: According to Aristotle, the forms of material things in the physical world are immaterial aspects of them. In addition, the material world, of which we are a part, includes an immaterial element because we have minds as well as brains, minds that are distinct from brains.

These are Aristotle's answers to the first two of the three difficult philosophical questions with which we began. The third and most difficult question—about the existence of a totally immaterial being—will be answered in the following chapter.

23

God

Aristotle's view of the universe as eternal—as everlastingly undergoing change—leads him to question the cause of everlasting change. He attributes all the changes constantly occurring on earth to the motion of the heavenly bodies. But what keeps them everlastingly in motion?

It cannot be something that is itself in motion or changing in any way. If it were, it, too, would need a cause of its motion, a cause of its changing. Given infinite time, one might go back from effect to cause in an infinite series and never reach a first cause—a mover in motion that is not itself moved by something else in motion.

A prime mover that moves everything that is in motion without moving and without being moved, must cause motion by being attractive rather than propulsive. The bat that hits the ball and propels it is the efficient or active cause of the ball's motion. The candy in the window that entices me into the store to buy and eat it causes my motion in a different way. Without itself moving, it attracts me. It is not the efficient but the final cause of my entering the store—the reason why I move in that direction.

To move everything else without itself being moved or in motion, the prime mover, Aristotle argues, must function as an attractive or final cause. In thinking this, he did not have in mind the gravitational attraction that the earth exerts upon the bodies that fall to its surface, or the gravitational attraction that the moon exerts upon the tides.

In his view, attractive or final causes operate on intelligences that can respond to them and adopt them as motives for action. When he says that a heavy body that falls to earth wishes to come to rest there, he is speaking metaphorically, not literally. That motion is only *like* the motion of the person that is attracted by the candy in the window to enter the store.

Thinking in this way, Aristotle found it necessary to endow the heavenly bodies with intelligences that function as their motors. As the engine of an automobile is its motor, so an intelligence is the motor that keeps a star in motion. But unlike the automobile engine, which must itself be set in motion, the celestial intelligences function as motors through being attracted by the prime mover of the universe.

To be an unmoved and eternal mover of a universe everlastingly in motion, the prime mover must be immutable. But to be immutable, in Aristotle's view, it must also be immaterial. Anything that is material has potentialities: it is subject to change or motion. It is also imperfect, for at any time it is not actually all that it can be.

We have seen, in earlier chapters, that that which is purely or completely potential cannot exist. Nothing exists that is not actual in some respects, while being potential in other respects. The reverse, however, is not true. Pure actuality (form without matter) can exist, though pure potentiality (matter without form) cannot.

It is by such reasoning that Aristotle came to the conclusion that the prime mover is pure actuality—a being totally devoid of matter or potentiality. In addition, this immaterial being is a perfect being, a being lacking no perfection that remains for it to attain. This perfect being, which is the prime mover of the universe, Aristotle called God.

God, for Aristotle, is not the only immaterial being in the universe. The intelligences that keep the stars in their eternal rounds through being attracted by the perfection of God are also immaterial. But though they, too, are immaterial in Aristotle's theory, he did not regard them as perfect or pure actualities. Only God is that.

It is difficult if not impossible to explain the potentiality that must be attributed to the stellar intelligences if they are not pure actualities. Something that is both immaterial and has potentiality does not fit easily into Aristotle's scheme of things.

To modern ears, Aristotle's account of what keeps the universe everlastingly in motion sounds mythical. Yet it is interesting to follow the reasoning that led him to affirm the existence of the immaterial and perfect being that he called God. That reasoning provided a model for later thinkers in their efforts to prove the existence of God—not Aristotle's God, but the God of Genesis, the God who created the world out of nothing.

The conception of God as Prime Mover and the conception of God as Creator are alike in three respects: the immateriality, the immutability, and the perfection of the Divine Being. But Aristotle's Prime Mover only serves to account for the eternity of the universe and its everlasting motion. It was the need to explain that which led Aristotle to develop his theory of the motion of the heavenly bodies and his concept of the Prime Mover as the final cause of their movements.

Aristotle did not think it necessary to explain the existence of the universe. Being eternal, it never came into existence, and so, in his view, it did not need an efficient cause that brought it into being—a cause that operated like a human maker who produces a work of art. We ordinarily speak of the human being who makes something as creative. However, the human creator always has the materials of nature to work on. He does not make something out of nothing. He is, therefore, not creative in the way that God is thought to be creative.

The conception of God as Creator arose from the need to explain the existence of the universe, as the conception of God as Prime Mover arose in Aristotle's mind from the need to explain the eternity of the universe and its everlasting motion. It is difficult to determine whether the conception of God as Creator would have arisen in the minds of later thinkers in the West had it not been for the opening sentence of Genesis, which reads, "In the beginning God created the heavens and the earth." This is regarded as divinely revealed truth by the three major religions of the West—Judaism, Christianity, and Islam.

It would be both natural and reasonable to ask whether Aristotle would have accepted or rejected what is asserted by that sentence. Since he thought the universe to be eternal, would he not have denied that the universe had a beginning? And, denying that, would he not also have rejected the notion of a God who created it?

If to create is to cause something that does not exist to come into existence (comparable to what the human artist does in producing a work of art), then a world that has no beginning does not need a creator. But even a world that has no beginning may need a cause for its continued existence if its existence is not necessary. Something that does not necessarily exist, in Aristotle's view, is something that may or may not exist. If the world does not exist necessarily, it may cease to exist. What, then, keeps a world that may cease to exist everlastingly in existence?

Aristotle did not himself raise or face that question. If he had, he might have reasoned his way to the conclusion that a cause was needed to keep the universe everlastingly in existence, just as he did reason his way to the conclusion that a cause was needed to keep the universe everlastingly in motion. By a slight shift in the meaning of the word "creator," the conclusion so reached might have led to the conception of God as Creator, not just as Prime Mover.

In one sense of the word, to create is to cause something that does not exist to come into existence. In another sense of the word (a more subtle sense, perhaps), to create is to cause the existence of that which may or may not exist, without regard to its coming into existence. It is in the latter, more subtle sense of the word that Aristotle might have conceived God both as Prime Mover and as Creator.

The Aristotelian theories described in this chapter and the theory that I have suggested he might have developed within the framework of his philosophy are not common sense. They are not even refinements of common sense, though they may be based on such refinements.

In this very important respect, the theories dealt with in this chapter differ from the philosophical views we have considered in earlier chapters of this book. The theories dealt with in this chapter might be regarded as Aristotle's theology, not his philosophy. If his theology is not related to our common-sense thought, as his philosophy is, it is at least related to common religious beliefs—religious beliefs that have prevailed in Western civilization for more than two thousand years. This fact is my reason for thinking that Aristotle's conception of God, and the reasoning that led him to develop it, should be included in this book.

Epilogue

For Those Who Have Read
or Who Wish to Read
Aristotle

In my Introduction to this book, I recommended to anyone who wished to learn how to think philosophically that Aristotle was the teacher to begin with. I did not recommend that anyone should start by reading the books that Aristotle wrote. That is the very last thing I would tell anyone to do.

Aristotle's books are much too difficult for beginners. Even in the best translations, much of what is said remains obscure. The translators use many words that are unfamiliar, words that we do not use in our everyday speech. Though some of the Greek words that Aristotle himself used were words that his fellow Greeks used, he gave them special meanings.

Nevertheless, some readers of this book may wish to read those parts of Aristotle's works from which I have drawn the inspiration for this exposition of his thoughts. It is even possible that among the readers of this book there will be some who have read the words of Aristotle before—if not in their entirety, at least certain of his major treatises. They may wish to check my exposition against the texts on which I have relied for the main tenets of Aristotle's thought.

To both groups of readers, I must confess that I have simplified wherever possible. I have substituted commonplace words for unusual ones. I have kept to the main thrust of Aristotle's thought on major points of his doctrine and have never allowed myself to be drawn off the main path by the qualifications, the complications, and the subtleties that Aristotle himself introduces, often to the perplexity rather than the enlightenment of his readers.

To provide those who have read or who wish to read Aristotle with a guide to the texts that have served as my sources, I have drawn up a second table of contents for this book, which parallels the table of contents that appears at its beginning. In this second table of contents, I have changed all the titles, substituting for the originals (which were appropriate to the style and substance of my rendition of Aristotle's thought) a set of titles that more precisely describes the Aristotelian doctrines being expounded in the five parts of this book and each of its twenty-three chapters.

To make this clear, I have placed in brackets, after the more precisely descriptive titles, the titles that appear in the table of contents at the beginning of this book. Under the title of each of the twenty-three chapters, I will sometimes place brief statements, in Aristotelian language, of the doctrines being expounded in that chapter. In every case, I will append a list of references to appropriate portions of Aristotle's works, in some cases indicating the special relevance of a particular portion being cited.

Part I. Aristotle's Universe of Discourse: His Categories and His Taxonomy [Man the Philosophical Animal]

1. *Aristotle's Fourfold Classification of Sensible,*

*Material Substances: Inorganic Bodies, Plants,
Animals, Men* [Philosophical Games]

In this chapter we are concerned with the criteria
by which Aristotle distinguished between living
and nonliving things; within the domain of living
things, between plants and animals; and within
the domain of animal life, between brute animals
and rational animals, i.e., human beings.

Metaphysics, Bk. I, Ch. 1.
On the soul, Bk. I, Chs. 1, 5; Bk. II, Chs. 1–3, 5,
    9; Bk. III, Chs. 3, 12.
History of Animals, Bk. X, Ch. 1.
Generation of Animals, Bk. I, Chs. 1–9; Book
    IV, Chs. 4–6.
Parts of Animals, Bk. I, Chs. 4–5.

It is also pointed out that Aristotle was aware of
difficulties in applying this scheme of classification. The difficulties arise because of the existence
of borderline cases that straddle the lines that
divide the living from the nonliving, and plants
from animals.

History of Animals, Bk. VIII, Ch. 1.

The distinction between essential and accidental
differences is introduced.

Categories, Ch. 5.
Metaphysics, Bk. V, Chs. 4, 11; Bk. IX, Ch. 8.

2. *The Range of Beings: The Ten Categories*
[The Great Divide]

In this chapter we are concerned with the being
of objects that do not exist in the way that sensible, material substances exist (e.g., mathematical objects, fictions, minds, ideas, immaterial
substances, such as the disembodied intelligences
that are the celestial motors, and God).

Metaphysics, Bk. III, Chs. 5–6; Bk. XII, Ch. 8;
   Bk. XIII, Chs. 1–5.
On the Heavens, Bk. II, Chs. 1, 12.
On the Soul, Bk. III, 4–6.

The distinction between substance and accident,
i.e., between bodies and their attributes.

Categories, Chs. 5–7.
Physics, Bk. I, Ch. 2.
Metaphysics, Bk. VII, Chs. 4–6.

The foregoing distinction is related to the point
that material substances are the subjects of
change, and their accidents are the respects in
which they change.

Physics, Bk. I, Chs. 6–7; Bk. II, Ch. 3.

Essence or specific nature in relation to substantial form.

Metaphysics, Bk. V, Chs. 4, 11; Bk. VII, Ch.
   16–VIII, Ch. 6; Bk. IX, Ch. 8.
On the Soul, Bk. II, Ch. 4.

The hierarchy of specific natures or essences.

Metaphysics, Bk. VIII, Ch. 3.
On the Soul, Bk. II, Ch. 3.

Aristotle's inventory of the various categories
under which the accidental attributes of substance fall.

Categories, Ch. 4.

Among the accidents of substance, some are
permanent or unchanging; these are the prop-
erties that are inseparable from the essential nature of each kind of material substance.

Topics, Bk. V, Chs. 1–3.

Aristotle's policy with regard to the ambiguity of words.

On Interpretation, Ch. 1.
Topics, Bk. II, Ch. 4.

3. Productive, Practical, and Theoretic Reason or Mind [Man's Three Dimensions]

This chapter briefly summarizes Aristotle's three-fold division of intellectual activity or thought into thought for the sake of making things, thought for the sake of moral and political action, and thought for the sake of acquiring knowledge as an end in itself.

Ethics, Bk. VI, Chs. 2, 4.
On the Soul, Bk. III, Ch. 7.

Part II. Aristotle's Philosophy of Nature and of Art [Man the Maker]

4. Nature as an Artist and the Human Artist as Imitator of Nature [Aristotle's Crusoe]

The difference between what happens by nature and what happens by art.

Physics, Bk. I, Chs. 7–8; Bk. II, Chs. 1–3, 8–9.
Poetics, Chs. 1–4.

The difference between what happens by art and what happens by chance.

Physics, Bk. II, Chs. 4–6.
Politics, Bk. I, Ch. 11.

The difference between the changes brought about by nature and the changes brought about by art.

Metaphysics, Bk. VII, Chs. 7–9.

The difference between man's production of corporeal things and the generation or procreation of living things in nature.

Generation of Animals
Metaphysics, Bk. VII, Ch. 7.

5. *The Three Main Modes of Accidental Change: Change of Place, Change of Quality, Change of Quantity* [Change of Permanence]

The distinction between substantial change and accidental change, and the differentiation of three distinct modes of accidental change.

Categories, Ch. 14.
Physics, Bk. III, Ch. 1; Bk. V, Chs. 1–2, 5; Bk. VII, Ch. 4; Bk. VIII, Ch. 7.

Corporeal substances as the permanent or enduring subjects that persist throughout all accidental changes.

Physics, Bk. I, Chs. 6–7; Bk. II, Chs. 1–3.
Metaphysics, Bks. VIII–IX; Bk. XII, Chs. 1–5.

Aristotle's refutation of the Parmenidean denial of change and of the Heraclitean denial of permanence.

Physics, Bk. I, Chs. 2–4, 8–9; Bk. VI, Ch. 9.

The Aristotelian distinction between natural and violent motion.

Physics, Bk. IV, Chs. 1, 8; Bk. V, Ch. 6; Bk. VIII, Ch. 4.
On the Heavens, Bk. I, Chs. 2–3, 7–8.

The special character of the subject of change in

generation and corruption: prime matter as the subject in substantial change.

Physics, Bk. I, Ch. 7; Bk. II, Chs. 1–3.
Metaphysics, Bk. VII, Chs. 7–9; Bk. XI, Ch. 11; Bk. XII, Chs. 2–3.

6. *Aristotle's Doctrine of the Four Causes: Efficient, Material, Formal, and Final* [The Four Causes]

The doctrine stated.

Physics, Bk. II, Chs. 3–9.
Metaphysics, Bk. I, Chs. 3–10; Bk. V, Ch. 3; Bk. VI, Chs. 2–3; Bk. VII, Ch. 17; Bk. VIII, Chs. 2–4; Bk. IX, Ch. 8; Bk. XII, Chs. 4–5.

The consideration of final causes in nature and art.

Physics, Bk. II, Chs. 8–9.
On the Soul, Bk. II, Chs. 12–13.
Parts of Animals, Bks. II–IV.
Generation of Animals, Bk. I, Chs. 4–13.

The role of potentiality and actuality in both substantial and accidental change.

Physics, Bk. III, Chs. 1–3.
Metaphysics, Bk. I, Chs. 6–7; Bk. VII, Chs. 3, 7–17; Bk. VIII, Chs. 4–6; Bk. XII, Chs. 2–5.

The role of substance as the material cause and of accidental form as the formal cause in accidental change; and of prime matter as the material cause and substantial form as the formal cause in substantial change.

Physics, Bk. I, Chs. 4–9; Bk. II, Ch. 7; Bk. II, Ch. 3.

Metaphysics, Bk. I, Chs. 6–7; Bk. V, Ch. 8; Bk. VII, Chs. 3, 7–17; Bk. VIII, Chs. 4–6; Bk. IX, Chs. 6–9; Bk. XII, Chs. 2–5.

7. *Further Developments in the Theory of Potentiality and Actuality, and of Matter and Form, Especially with Respect to Substantial Change, or Generation and Corruption* [To Be and Not to Be]

Physics, Bk. III, Chs. 1–3.
Metaphysics, Bk. VII, Chs. 6–9; Bk. IX, Chs. 1, 3–9; Bk. XI, 9, 11; Bk. XII, 2–3, 5.
Generation and Corruptions, Bk. I, Chs. 1, 3–5; Bk. II, Chs. 1, 7, 9.

8. *Aristotle's Analysis of the Intellectual Factors in Artistic Production and His Classification of the Arts* [Productive Ideas and Know-How]

The intellectual virtue of art.

Ethics, Bk. VI, Ch. 4.

The artist as imitator.

Poetics, Chs. 1–5.

The special character of the three cooperative arts of farming, healing, and teaching.

Physics, Bk. II, Chs. 1–2, 8.

The beauty of products that are well made.

Poetics, Ch. 7.

Part III. Aristotle's Moral and Political Philosophy [Man the Doer]

9. *The End as the First Principle in Practical*

Thinking and the Use of Means as the Beginning of Action: The End as First in the Order of Intention and Last in the Order of Execution [Thinking about Ends and Means]

The good as the desirable and the desirable as the good.

Ethics, Bk. I, Chs. 1–2.

The distinction between ends and means as goods desirable for their own sake and goods desirable for the sake of something else.

Ethics, Bk. I, Chs. 5, 7, 9.

The ultimate end in practical thinking compared with axioms or self-evident truths in theoretical thinking.

Posterior Analytics, Bk. I, Ch. 2.

10. *Happiness Conceived as That Which Leaves Nothing to Be Desired and, as so Conceived, the Final or Ultimate End to Be Sought* [Living and Living Well]

The distinction between living and living well.

Politics, Bk. I, Chs. 1–2, 9.

The conception of happiness as a whole good life, together with various views held by individuals concerning what a good life consists in.

Ethics, Bk. I, Chs. 4–5, 7–10; Bk. X, Chs. 2, 6–8.

11. *Aristotle's Distinction Between Real and Apparent Goods, or Between Goods That Ought to Be Desired and Goods That Are in Fact Desired, Together with His Distinction Between*

Natural and Acquired Desires [Good, Better, Best]

Ethics, Bk. II, Ch. 6; Bk. III, Chs. 4–5; Bk. X, Ch. 5.
On the Soul, Bk. II, Chs. 2–3; Bk. III, Chs. 3, 7.
Rhetoric, Bk. I, Chs. 6–7.

12. *The Real Goods That Are the Components of the Whole of Goods That Constitute Happiness, and Moral Virtue as Indispensable to the Pursuit of Happiness* [How to Pursue Happiness]

Ethics, Bk. I, Chs. 4–5, 7–10; Bk. VII, Chs. 11–14; Bk. IX, Chs. 4, 8–11; Bk. X, Chs. 1–8.

13. *Moral Virtue and Good Fortune as the Two Indispensable Operative Factors in the Pursuit of Happiness* [Good Habits and Good Luck]

Moral virtue in general and the three main aspects of moral virtue: temperance, courage, and justice.

Ethics, Bks. II–V.

Good fortune as indispensable to happiness: the distinction between the virtuous and the blessed man.

Ethics, Bk. I, Ch. 10; Bk. VII, Ch. 13; Bk. X, Ch. 8.
Politics, Bk. VII, Chs. 1, 13.

The distinction between limited and unlimited goods: moral virtue as resulting in moderation with respect to limited goods.

Ethics, Bk. VII, Ch. 14.
Politics, Bk. I, Chs. 8–10; Bk. VII, Ch. 1.

14. *The Obligations of the Individual With Re-*

gard to the Happiness of Others and With Regard to the Welfare of the Organized Community [What Others Have a Right to Expect from Us]

Man as a social and political animal.

Politics, Bk. I, Chs. 1–2.

The family, the tribe, and the state, or political society, as organized communities.

Politics, Bk. I, Chs. 1–2.

Justice as moral virtue directed toward the good of others.

Ethics, Bk. V, Chs. 1–2.

The distinction between justice, on the one hand, and friendship or love, on the other.

Ethics, Bk. VIII, Chs. 1, 9.

The kinds of friendship.

Ethics, Bk. VIII, Chs. 2–6.

15. *The Role of the State in Abetting or Facilitating the Individual's Pursuit of Happiness* [What We Have a Right to Expect from Others and from the State]

Aristotle's conception of the good state as one that promotes the pursuit of happiness by its citizens.

Politics, Bk. I, Ch. 2; Bk. II, Ch. 6; Bk. III, Chs. 9–10; Bk. VII, Chs. 1–3, 13–14.

Aristotle's theory of the forms of government, and of the criteria for judging the goodness and badness of diverse forms of government.

Politics, Bk. I, Chs. 1, 5, 12–13; Bk. III, Chs. 6–7, 11, 15–16; Bk. V, Chs. 2–3, 8, 12; Bk. VI, Ch. 4; Bk. VII, Chs. 2, 14.

Aristotle's distinction between natural and legal or conventional slavery.

Politics, Bk. I, Chs. 4–7, 13.

Aristotle's theory of natural as distinct from legal or conventional justice.

Ethics, Bk. V, Ch. 7.

Aristotle's view of the role of women in the family and the state.

Politics, Bk. I, Ch. 13.

Part IV. Aristotle's Psychology, Logic, and Theory of Knowledge [Man the Knower]

16. *The Senses and the Intellect: Perception, Memory, Imagination, and Conceptual Thought* [What Goes into the Mind and What Comes out of It]

Language in relation to thought.

Categories, Ch. 1.
On Interpretation, Chs. 1–2.

Aristotle's account of the external senses and of their distinction from the interior senses: the common sense, memory, and imagination.

On the Soul, Bk. II, Chs. 5–12; Bk. III, Chs. 1–3.
Sense and the Sensible
History of Animals, Bk. IV, Ch. 8.

The distinction between mere sensations and perceptual experience.

Metaphysics, Bk. I, Ch. 1.

Aristotle's doctrine that sensations and ideas, taken by themselves or in isolation, are neither true nor false.

Categories, Ch. 4.
On Interpretation, Ch. 1.
On the Soul, Bk. II, Ch. 6; Bk. III, Chs. 3, 6.
Metaphysics, Bk. IV, Ch. 5; Bk. V, Ch. 29.

Aristotle's theory of ideas as forms that the intellect abstracts from experience.

On the Soul, Bk. III, Chs. 4, 7–8.
Metaphysics, Bk. XIII, Chs. 2–3.

17. *Immediate Inference and Syllogistic Reasoning* [Logic's Little Words]

The law of contradiction as an ontological principle and as a rule of thought.

On Interpretation, Ch. 6.
Prior Analytics, Bk. II, Ch. 17.
Posterior Analytics, Bk. I, Ch. 11.
Metaphysics, Bk. IV, Chs. 3–8; Bk. IX, Chs. 5–6.

The square of opposition: contradictories, contraries, and subcontraries.

On Interpretation, Chs. 6, 10.
Categories, Ch. 10.
Prior Analytics, Bk. I, Ch. 2.

Immediate inference based on the square of opposition.

On Interpretation, Chs. 7–10.
Prior Analytics, Bk. I, Chs. 2–3; Bk. II, Chs. 8–10, 22.

The rules of the syllogism.

Prior Analytics, Bk. I.
Posterior Analytics, Bk. I, Ch. 12.

Aristotle's distinction between logical validity and factual truth.

Prior Analytics, Bk. II, Chs. 2–4.
Posterior Analytics, Bk. I, Ch. 12.

The enthymeme in rhetorical argument.

Prior Analytics, Bk. II, Ch. 27.
Rhetoric, Bk. II, Chs. 20, 22.

18. *Theoretical and Practical Truth* [Telling the Truth and Thinking It]

The definition of truth.

Metaphysics, Bk. IV, Ch. 7.
Categories, Ch. 5.

The truth of axioms or first principles: self-evident truths.

Posterior Analytics, Bk. I, Chs. 3, 5, 10, 12.

Sentences that are neither true nor false.

On Interpretation, Ch. 2.

Aristotle's theory of the difference between the truth of factual and of normative statements: "is-statements" and "ought-statements."

Ethics, Bk. VI, Ch. 2.

The certitude or probability with which propositions are affirmed or denied.

On Interpretation, Ch. 9.
Prior Analytics, Bk. I, Ch. 13; Bk. II, Ch. 25.
Posterior Analytics, Bk. I, Chs. 2, 6, 8, 30, 33.
Metaphysics, Bk. IV, Chs. 4–6; Bk. VI, Ch. 1;
Bk. IX, Chs. 6–7.

19. *Aristotle's Theory of Knowledge and His
Distinction Between Knowledge and Right Opinion* [Beyond a Reasonable Doubt]

Categories, Ch. 5.
Prior Analytics, Bk. I, Ch. 13.
Posterior Analytics, Bk. I, Chs. 2, 4–8, 30, 33.
Topics, Bk. I, Ch. 2.
Rhetoric, Bk. II, Ch. 25.
Metaphysics, Bk. IV, Ch. 4; Bk. VI, Ch. 2; Bk.
VII, Ch. 15; Bk. IX, Ch. 10; Bk. XI, Chs.
6, 8.
On the Soul, Bk. III, Ch. 3.

Part V. Aristotle's Cosmology and Theology [Difficult
Philosophical Questions]

20. *The Actual and the Potential Infinite* [In-
finity]

Aristotle's criticism of the theory of the atomists.

Physics, Bk. I, Ch. 2.
On the Heavens, Bk. III, Ch. 4; Bk. IV, Ch. 2.

Aristotle's doctrine with regard to the infinite
divisibility of continuous magnitudes and of
matter.

Physics, Bk. III, Chs. 1, 6–7; Bk. V, Ch. 3; Bk.
VI, Chs. 1–2.

Metaphysics, Bk. III, Ch. 4; Bk. V, Ch. 13.

Aristotle's denial of actually infinite multitudes or magnitudes, together with his affirmation of the potential infinites of addition or division.

Physics, Bk. III, Chs. 4–8.
Metaphysics, Bk. XI, Ch. 10.

21. *The Eternity of the World and of Motion or Change* [Eternity]

Aristotle's conception of time as the measure of motion.

Physics, Bk. IV, Chs. 10–14.

Aristotle's arguments for the endlessness of time and for the everlastingness of motion or change.

Physics, Bk. VII, Chs. 1–2; Bk. VIII, Chs. 1–6, 8.

Aristotle's theory of the influence of the motion of the heavens upon terrestrial motions and changes.

On the Heavens, Bk. I, Chs. 2, 9–12; Bk. II, Ch. 3.
Generation and Corruption, Bk. II, Chs. 10–11.

Aristotle's conception of the immutability or eternity of God: the timelessness of the eternal or immutable.

Metaphysics, Bk. XII, Chs. 6–7, 9.

22. *The Immateriality of the Human Intellect: Conceptual Thought as Involving the Abstraction of Forms From Matter* [The Immateriality of Mind]

Posterior Analytics, Bk. I, Ch. 3.

On the Soul, Bk. III, Chs. 4–5, 7–8.
Metaphysics, Bk. XIII, Chs. 2–3.

23. *The Prime Mover: The Divine Being as Pure Actuality* [God]

Aristotle's theory of intelligences as celestial motors.

On the Heavens, Bk. II, Chs. 1, 12.
Metaphysics, Bk. XII, Ch. 8.

Aristotle's arguments for the existence of a prime mover that causes the motion of the heavens in the matter of a final, not an efficient, cause.

Physics, Bk. VIII, Chs. 1–6.
Metaphysics, Bk. XII, Chs. 6–9.

ABOUT THE AUTHOR

MORTIMER J. ADLER is the chairman of Britannica's Board of Editors, director of the Institute for Philosophical Research, and senior associate of the Aspen Institute for Humanistic Studies, of which he was one of the founders. He is the author of the well known *How to Read a Book*, *Philosopher at Large*, his intellectual autobiography; *How to Think About God*; and coeditor, with Charles Van Doren, of *Great Treasury of Western Thought*, declared the reference book of 1977 by the American Library Association.

BANTAM NEW AGE BOOKS

Bantam New Age Books are for all those interested in reflecting on life today and life as it may be in the future. This important new imprint features stimulating works in fields from biology and psychology to philosophy and the new physics.

☐	13578	**THE DANCING WU LI MASTERS:**	$3.95
		An Overview of the New Physics Gary Zukav	
☐	14131	**THE FIRST THREE MINUTES** Steven Weinberg	$2.95
☐	13470	**LIFETIDE** Lyall Watson	$3.50
☐	12478	**MAGICAL CHILD** Joseph Chilton Pearce	$3.50
☐	13406	**THE MEDUSA AND THE SNAIL** Lewis Thomas	$2.95
☐	13724	**MIND AND NATURE:** A Necessary Unity	$3.50
		Gregory Bateson	
☐	20322	**HEALTH FOR THE WHOLE PERSON**	$3.95
		James Gordon	
☐	20708	**ZEN/MOTORCYCLE MAINTENANCE**	$3.95
		Robert Pirsig	
☐	12813	**THE SCIENTIST** Lilly, M.D.	$2.95
☐	10949	**TO HAVE OR TO BE** Fromm	$2.95
☐	14821	**IN THE SHINING MOUNTAINS**	$3.95
		David Thomson	
☐	14526	**FOCUSING** Eugene Gendlin	$3.50
☐	13972	**LIVES OF A CELL** Lewis Thomas	$2.95
☐	14206	**TAO OF PHYSICS** Fritjof Capra	$3.95
☐	14353	**WINE OF LIFE & OTHER ESSAYS**	$2.95
		Harold Morowitz	

Buy them at your bookstore or use this handy coupon for ordering:

Bantam Books, Inc., Dept. NA, 414 East Golf Road, Des Plaines, Ill. 60016

Please send me the books I have checked above. I am enclosing $_____
(please add $1.00 to cover postage and handling). Send check or money order
—no cash or C.O.D.'s please.

Mr/Mrs/Miss_____

Address_____

City_____ State/Zip_____

NA—1/82
Please allow four to six weeks for delivery. This offer expires 6/82.